Radical Self-Love

Healing from Toxic Relationships

An Workbook to Guide You on Your Path of Self-Love

TANISHA DUKE-SCORZA

Copyright PAGE

COPYRIGHT © TENDER LOVE SUPPORT, LLC

THIS DOCUMENT IS FOR PERSONAL USE ONLY.

IT MAY NOT BE REPRODUCED, DISTRIBUTED, OR SHARED WITHOUT WRITTEN PERMISSION FROM TANISHA SCORZA

GRAPHICS IN THIS DOCUMENT WERE CREATED BY TANISHA SCORZA and OTHER ARTIST

THIS IS FOR MOTIVATIONAL PURPOSES ONLY.

© TENDER LOVE AND SUPPORT

Table of Contents

MESSAGE FROM A GODDESS * 5

INTRODUCTION * 7

RADICAL SELF LOVE JOURNEY

UNDERSTANDING SELF * 11

ACCEPTANCE * 18

COMMUNICATION * 22

CREATING HEALTHY HABITS * 26

SETTING BOUNDARIES * 31

DEEP REFLECTION * 35

ENGAGING IN POSITIVE SELF-TALK * 41

PRACTICING GOOD SELF-CARE * 52

BECOMING MINDFUL * 62

RADICAL SELF-LOVE * 68

RESOURCES

PRAYER AFFIRMATION * 77

REFLECTION NOTE SHEETS * 78

DAILY TASK SHEETS * 84

SMART GOALS * 90

SWOT ANALYSIS * 95

HABIT TRACKER * 97

AFFIRMATION * 105

ABOUT THE AUTHOR * 107

With every breath, you ascend further into your truth. This is your sacred transformation.

A Message from the Heart of the Goddess

While this is not the entirety of my story—perhaps a book will follow—it is a reflection of the goddess within me, who dances gracefully between the realms of light and shadow.

I have learned to honor the balance in life, expressing gratitude for the echoes of my actions, For I have come to realize, that the life I live, is the outcome of the choices I make.

I chose to change. I chose to break free from the toxic entanglements of past desires that no longer aligned with my true self. Through this journey of transformation, I have uncovered my most authentic self, shining brightly in the truth of who I am.

It is my deepest wish that this workbook serves as a guiding light for you, leading you to your own sacred path of self-discovery. May it help you embrace the goddess within and uncover your most authentic self,

Just as I have found mine.

Let this be your invitation to rise, heal, and shine in the fullness of your divine essence.

This sacred book was created with the hope that my journey will inspire and empower you to fall deeply in love with yourself.

With divine love and light,

Tanisha Duke-Scorza

xxx

Website: www.tenderlovesupport.com

With each step, you ascend. With each breath, you blossom. This is your divine transformation.

Introduction

Welcome to Your Sacred Journey: A Guide to Radical Self-Love

Greetings, Divine Being, and welcome to the beginning of your sacred journey of healing, transformation, and deep self-love. Radical Self-Love: Healing from Toxic Relationships is more than just a workbook book—it is a divine tool, designed to help you reconnect with your inner power, reclaim your self-worth, and begin the process of healing from the toxic patterns that no longer serve your highest good. This reflection guide is your gentle companion, offering you sacred space to explore, reflect, and grow into the fullness of who you are.

As you hold this book in your hands, know that you are holding the key to unlock the parts of yourself that long for your attention, care, and love. This workbook is for the soul seeking clarity, for the heart ready to heal, and for the mind that craves understanding. It is crafted for those who feel the call to begin their healing journey but are unsure where to start—especially for those considering therapy but need guidance on what to focus on.

With each activity, you will dive deeper into the layers of your being, uncovering truths, confronting patterns, and ultimately embracing the beautiful essence of who you are. Whether you are already in therapy or just beginning your self-discovery, this workbook will help you identify the areas in your life that need attention and love.

So, gather your favorite pens or colored pencils, find a comfortable space, and prepare to engage in a transformative process. This is your time to honor yourself, to heal, and to love yourself completely. This is your season of healing!

How to Use This Activity Book

Each reflection in this book is intentionally designed to guide you on a journey of self-exploration. As you move through the exercises, you'll be invited to reflect on your life, your patterns, your inner thoughts, and your relationships. You will uncover areas where love and healing are needed, and where your soul craves attention.

Take your time as you work through each reflection exercise. There is no rush, and no right or wrong way to engage with this material. Each section is crafted to meet you where you are. Some reflections may be light and joyful, while others may take you deep into the core of your emotions. Honor your pace and be gentle with yourself throughout the process. allow yourself to be vulnerable

As you move through the book, you may find that it also serves as a tool to gain deeper insight into your healing journey, especially as you prepare for or engage in therapy. By identifying the areas of your life where love is most needed, you can enter therapy with a clearer understanding of what you wish to focus on.

Introduction Cont.

The 10 Sacred Reflections of Radical Self-Love:

1. Understanding Self
- The foundation of your healing journey begins with a deep understanding of yourself. In this activity, you will explore your values, passions, and the unique essence that makes you. You'll reflect on your identity—separate from external influences or toxic relationships—so you can reconnect with your true self. Understanding who you are is the first step toward loving yourself fully.

2. Acceptance
- In the divine act of self-love, acceptance is key. This activity will guide you toward radical acceptance—of your strengths, your weaknesses, and everything in between. It is through acceptance that we release self-judgment and begin to embrace ourselves in our entirety. You will explore what it means to be gentle with yourself, to forgive past mistakes, and to honor where you are on your journey.

3. Communication
- The way you communicate with yourself, and others shapes your relationships and your reality. This activity invites you to examine your patterns of communication—are you clear, loving, and honest with yourself? Do you communicate your needs to others in a healthy way? Through reflection and practical exercises, you'll begin to cultivate the type of communication that nurtures your inner being and fosters healthier connections with others.

4. Creating Healthy Habits
- Self-love is nurtured through the habits we practice daily. In this activity, you will reflect on the habits that serve you and those that do not. You'll create a new framework for daily living, one that supports your mental, emotional, and physical health. These habits are sacred rituals, designed to ground you, uplift you, and keep you aligned with your highest self.

5. Setting Boundaries
- Boundaries are an essential act of self-respect and protection. This activity will help you identify areas in your life where you need stronger boundaries and provide guidance on how to set them. You will reflect on the importance of boundaries in preserving your peace, your energy, and your well-being. Setting boundaries is an act of love—it is about teaching others how to treat you and creating space for your growth.

Introduction *Cont.*

6. Deep Reflection
- In this activity, you are invited to engage in deep inner reflection. This is where you confront past experiences, emotions, and patterns that may be blocking your self-love. You will explore past relationships and toxic dynamics, allowing you to gain insight into the lessons they brought and begin the healing process. Through journaling and introspection, you'll uncover truths that will guide you toward greater self-awareness.

7. Engaging in Positive Self-Talk
- How you speak to yourself shapes your inner world. This activity focuses on challenging negative self-talk and replacing it with positive affirmations. You will rewrite the script that runs in your mind, choosing words and thoughts that reflect your worth and potential. This exercise is about becoming your own biggest advocate, creating a mindset of love and support.

8. Practicing Good Self-Care
- Self-care is the physical embodiment of self-love. In this activity, you will design a self-care plan that nourishes your emotional, mental, physical, and spiritual well-being. You will reflect on what self-care looks like for you and how you can consistently prioritize yourself. This is your time to ensure that your needs are met and that you are cared for, every day.

9. Becoming Mindful
- Mindfulness invites you to be fully present in the moment, aware of your thoughts, emotions, and surroundings without judgment. In this activity, you will practice mindfulness techniques that help you stay grounded and connected to yourself. Whether through meditation, deep breathing, or simply paying attention to the present moment, you will cultivate a sense of peace and inner clarity.

10. Radical Self-Love
- The final activity brings everything together. This is where you declare your commitment to radical self-love. In this exercise, you will reflect on your journey, celebrate your growth, and affirm your intention to continue loving yourself fiercely and unconditionally. This activity is your opportunity to honor your path and step fully into your power as a being of love, deserving of the deepest care and compassion.

Introduction Cont.

Your Journey Awaits

Dear Goddess,

This book is your invitation to reconnect with your soul, to heal from the wounds of toxic relationships, and to embrace the fullness of who you are. Each activity is crafted to help you discover the power within and to guide you toward radical self-love.

Take your time, honor yourself, and know that every step you take on this journey is a step toward greater peace, healing, and joy. You are worthy of love, and this book will help you reclaim it. The love you seek is already within you—this activity book will help you uncover it.

Blessings and love on your journey.
You are divine.
You are whole.
You are loved.

Tanisha Duke-Scorza

Celebrate you

Reflection 1: Understanding Self

"Be you and they will adjust." unknown

My voyage of self-discovery has been nothing short of a sacred odyssey—a profound journey of introspection and awakening. As a woman, mother, and partner, I ventured deep within, peeling back the layers of my existence to uncover the truths that had long lain dormant beneath the surface of my soul.

This journey began with an exploration of my past, where I encountered the echoes of a young goddess—my 13- or 14-year-old self—who had once felt misunderstood, rejected, and overlooked by those she held closest to her heart. These echoes, though distant, had reverberated through the corridors of my life, influencing my reactions and shaping my responses to the challenges I faced. As I delved into the depths of my inner world, I came face to face with the dormant emotions and unresolved wounds that had been hidden away for so long. These were the echoes of my youthful experiences, manifesting as patterns of thought and behavior that no longer served me. But rather than shy away, I chose to embrace these vulnerabilities, to acknowledge the pain of the past, and to initiate a process of healing and transformation.

With each step I took on this sacred journey, I reclaimed pieces of my true essence. I began to reconnect with the divine goddess within me, who had been waiting patiently for me to return. Through the power of self-compassion, introspection, and personal growth, I have emerged from this journey stronger, wiser, and more in tune with the radiant light that shines from within—the light of a goddess reborn.

Tender Love Support, always, Tanisha Duke-Scorza

> *With each affirmation, you rise.*
> *With each breath, you embody your divine essence.*

INSTRUCTIONS

Understanding Self Activities:

In these sacred activities, I invite you to embark on a journey deep within, where the essence of your divine goddess patiently awaits her awakening. This is your time to rise. Through the soft embrace of your vulnerabilities, the acceptance of all that has shaped you, and the courageous steps toward transformation, you will discover the radiant light that has always lived within you. Just as the moon emerges from darkness, so too will you rise—reborn, empowered, and illuminated in your truest form. The goddess within you is ready to ascend.

I allow love to flow freely to and from me.

Protecting YOUR INNERCHILD

VISUALIZATION MEDTIATION

Close your eyes and journey within to the depths of your inner goddess. Envision yourself as a tender child of innocence, seeking love and solace in the vastness of existence. Peer into the eyes of this precious child and recognize the profound yearning within— a yearning for love, acceptance, and understanding.

Extend your arms with tenderness and embrace this inner child with pure love and compassion. Whisper words of adoration and affirmation, affirming her innate perfection and the beauty of her journey. Assure her that it's okay to feel vulnerable at times, and that mistakes are simply steppingstones towards growth and wisdom. Let her know that she is never alone, for your loving presence will forever surround her.

Now, visualize this radiant child merging seamlessly into your being, nestled gently within your heart. Place your hand upon your heart center, anchoring this profound connection. Make a solemn vow to always cherish and nurture this inner essence, promising to be her steadfast companion through life's ebbs and flows.

Activity: Take time to reflect on the emotions stirred within you by this sacred communion. What sensations arose? What insights and revelations did you encounter on this transformative journey of self-love and acceptance? Jot down your thoughts, by using one of the Reflection Note Sheet" located in the back of the book.

Why is Understanding yourself IMPORTANT

Understanding your true essence is the gateway to divine empowerment, authenticity, and inner tranquility. Through the sacred journey of self-awareness, you awaken to the unique gifts you possess, navigate life's waves with divine clarity, and cultivate a profound sense of purpose and fulfillment.

To begin this journey of introspection into your vulnerability, I invite you to take one of the Reflection Notes sheets located at the back of this sacred text. As you prepare to answer the questions provided, allow yourself to be fully present, embracing the wisdom that flows from within as you explore the depths of your divine vulnerability.

1. Being Vulnerable
In what ways can embracing your vulnerability reveal the deepest truths of your soul, allowing your divine light to shine more brightly?

2. Raw Vulnerability
How does the goddess within you respond when you are faced with moments of raw vulnerability, and what wisdom does she offer to guide you through?

3. Embracing Vulnerability
What sacred practices or rituals can you invoke to honor and protect your vulnerability, ensuring that it is seen as a source of strength rather than a weakness?

4. Vulnerability as a Bridge
How do you allow your vulnerability to serve as a bridge to deeper connections with others, inviting them into the sacred space of your authentic self?

5. Acknowledging your Vulnerabilities
In what ways does acknowledging your vulnerability empower you to transcend fear and embody the fullness of your divine feminine power?

Why is Understanding yourself IMPORTANT

Beloved, to truly embrace the essence of Radical Self-Love, it is essential to journey inward and direct your thoughts with purpose. Below are sacred examples of how to channel your inner wisdom and gain a deep understanding of what each question is calling forth from your soul:

Examples

1. Being Vulnerable
Radical Self-Acceptance: Allow Yourself to Be Seen: Nurture Self-Compassion: Trust Your Intuition: Release Control: Embrace Your Sacred Feminine

2. Raw Vulnerability
Surrender to the Moment: Compassion as a Shield: Courage in Transparency: Intuition as the North Star: Embrace the Sacred Feminine: Rise Through Reflection:

3. Embracing Vulnerability
Anointing with Sacred Oils: Daily Affirmations: Sacred Altar: Journaling: Moon and Candle Rituals:

4. Vulnerability as a Bridge
Lead with Authenticity: Hold Space without Judgement: Speak Your Truth, Even When It's Uncomfortable: Invite Intimacy: Acknowledge Connections: Release Fear of Rejection

5. Acknowledging your Vulnerabilities
Owning my story: Embracing the Power of Softness: Transcending Fear through Trust: Tapping into Intuition and Inner Wisdom: Breaking Free from Perfectionism: Create Space for Healing:

A Letter to... THE LITTLE ME

Activity: There are sacred truths your inner child yearns to hear for her spirit to feel at peace. Envision your younger self, a radiant girl of 6 to 10 years old. What words of love and wisdom would you offer her if you could step through the veil of time and hold her in your embrace? How could you empower her to honor herself by setting healthy boundaries even at such a tender age?

Dear:

I love you because...

You didn't deserve...

You did your best...

It's okay to...

You are going to be all right because...

A Letter to... THE LITTLE ME *Cont.*
Example

Now that you have unveiled your vulnerabilities lets connect with your inner child, it's time to write them a letter. This letter should reflect your promise to protect and honor their needs. Be compassionate and gentle in your words. Acknowledge the pain they've felt and offer them the love and protection they may not have received in the past.

Example Letter:

Dear Little Tanisha,

    I see you. I see the times you felt hurt, scared, unheard or misunderstood. I want you to know that I am here for you now. You no longer have to carry those burdens alone. I promise to protect you from harm, both from others and from the harsh ways I sometimes speak to myself. You are so loved, just as you are.

    From this day forward, I will honor your needs, your desires, and your dreams. I will be gentle with you, and I will make sure you feel safe. I will give you space to laugh, play, and be yourself without fear. You deserve the best of me, and I am committed to giving you that.

Tender Love Support, always,
Tanisha Duke-Scorza

Reflection 2:
Acceptance

"I learned when I judge I focus on what I don't want and what I don't want magnifies! ACCEPTANCES is SELF-LOVE" unknown.

In the sacred journey of learning acceptance, I found myself standing at the crossroads of inner strength and resilience, much like a goddess awakening to her divine power. It was within this transformative space—a space where light and shadow converge—that I began the delicate art of weaving boundaries around my sacred self.

Acceptance, as I came to understand, is not a passive act of surrender but rather an active, conscious choice to embrace reality with grace and wisdom. As I surrendered to this divine dance, a beautiful tapestry of choices began to unfurl before me. Each thread in this tapestry represented a decision, a step closer to the truth of who I am. Yet, as I looked upon this intricate creation, I noticed that the vibrant essence of my soul had been partially obscured by threads woven with love and commitment to others, especially my family. These threads, although crafted with the purest of intentions, were slowly suffocating the goddess within.

In a moment of profound clarity, a revelation washed over me—true empowerment does not come from self-sacrifice but from self-preservation. Like the first rays of dawn piercing the veil of night, this realization illuminated my path. I understood that I could save myself without abandoning those I love. In fact, by choosing to nurture my soul, I would empower my family to flourish even more brilliantly. My authentic radiance, once hidden, could now shine fully, not only illuminating my path but also guiding those I hold dear.

Tender Love Support, always, Tanisha Duke-Scorza

I love you, I love me, so, it is a divine order that you love me as well as you love you!

INSTRUCTIONS

Acceptance Activities:

The following activities calls you to journey within, to the sacred space where your highest self-resides. It is here that you will uncover the places within that long for acceptance and compassion. What thought or memory keeps you tethered to lower vibrations? Go there now, and with the power of your heart, offer it the love and acceptance it has been yearning for. Watch as your soul transforms, like the caterpillar embracing its metamorphosis, blossoming into the radiant butterfly of your true essence. This is your moment to ascend.

I honor my journey and the lessons it has brought me.

the Chain — I choose me!

Set the sacred timer for 5 minutes and step into the radiant aura of your highest self. What is that thought that feeds your procrastination? What is the thought that stops you from doing what you know would bring joy into your life? What is that belief? Does it serve you?

I choose Me

the Best FUTURE ME

Set the sacred timer for 5 minutes and step into the radiant aura of your highest self. Who is she, this goddess of your dreams? Envision the embodiment of your aspirations, the pinnacle of your desires. See her shining brightly in the tapestry of your future, adorned with the treasures of fulfillment and joy. Let your imagination dance with the essence of your best self, for in this moment, you are limitless, empowered, and divine.

BEST VERSION OF *Me*

Reflection 3: Communication

"Communication is the gas needed to keep the fire of love burning." unknown.

In the sacred odyssey of self-discovery and love, I found that internal communication became my guiding beacon, illuminating the path toward my truest self. This journey was a quest—a deeply sacred quest to commune with my body, to uncover the buried treasures of past traumas, and to gently peel back the intricate layers of self-denial that had long shrouded my divine essence. Within the deepest chambers of my being, I nurtured a profound love for my marriage and family, a love that was both fierce and tender. Yet, as an empath, I came to realize the vital need for boundaries, a necessity for preserving my own well-being amidst the energies of others.

As I delved deeper into introspection, engaging in sacred dialogue with my inner self, a revelation unfolded—a profound understanding that my body had been speaking to me all along, whispering the truths of a life not fully aligned with authentic love. The signs were there, woven into the fabric of my existence: the weight that clung stubbornly, the persistent gnawing of stress lodged deep within my core, the gradual shedding of hair—a silent narrative of neglect, a body crying out for the love and care it so desperately needed.

In the dance of motherhood and the sacred duties of a wife, I poured my love and energy generously, cherishing these roles that defined so much of my existence. Yet, in my devotion, I inadvertently forsook the vital act of nurturing myself. The whirlwind of family life engulfed me, leaving little space for the blossoming of self-care, for the gentle cultivation of self-love.

In this intricate dance, I found myself caught in the web of toxic positivity—a veneer of happiness that masked the turmoil within. I surrendered to the expectations, the emotions, the narratives of my loved ones, allowing their voices to drown out my own, to obscure my authentic self.

But then, with a clarity as sharp as a blade, I realized the truth that had been waiting for me: I needed to reclaim my autonomy. I needed to rediscover the sacred rhythm of my own voice, to prioritize my well-being alongside the souls I cherished. And so, I embarked on this journey anew, with the goddess within me as my guide, ready to honor both my needs and my love for those who share this sacred path with me.

Tender Love Support, always, Tanisha Duke-Scorza

INSTRUCTIONS

Communication Activity:

This activity calls you to reflect on the divine messages you constantly whisper to yourself. Your thoughts are sacred—they birth emotions and shape the reality around you. Take this moment to examine the thoughts you have allowed to blossom into your world. What truths, fears, or desires have you manifested into your reality? Embrace this awareness, for it is through conscious communication with yourself that you hold the power to create the life that honors your highest self.

I am in complete harmony with my soul's purpose.

What's on your Mind!

Embrace a transformative writing exercise by engaging in a dialogue with your inner goddess. Begin by asking yourself profound questions like, "Who are you?" and "Where am I deceiving myself?" Take this opportunity to transmute any deceptions into empowering affirmations, reshaping apprehensions into clear objectives and aspirations that align with your highest self. Embrace this sacred journey of self-discovery and empowerment through radical self-love.

Here is an example of a <u>deceptive thought</u>: *"I am a procrastinator."*
<u>Affirmation</u>: *I honor my natural flow and trust that I act in perfect timing. I release the label of procrastination and embrace my power to create, move, and manifest when aligned with my highest purpose. I am in harmony with my journey, and all unfolds as it should.*

DECEPTION:

AFFIRMATION:

DECEPTION:

AFFIRMATION:

DECEPTION:

AFFIRMATION:

Mental Health Break:

Reflection:

How do you feel? What shifts have you noticed within your mind, body, and soul? Acknowledge any reflections or emotions that surface as you continue your journey of radical self-love. Embrace this sacred process, by journaling, doodling or drawing.

Grab a cup of tea and let your mind be free!

Reflection 4:
Creating Healthy Habits

"I take a day to slowdown &recharge my spirit resting feels good." unknown

In the sacred dance of family life, there were moments when I found myself struggling to maintain healthy habits, particularly as a devoted wife, deeply honoring the presence of my husband in our shared sanctuary. Yet, as I turned inward and embarked on a profound journey of self-discovery, a realization dawned upon me—the energy he brought into our home no longer resonated with the essence of the goddess I was becoming.

His dominant presence had subtly infiltrated every corner of our life together, casting a shadow over my spirit, and stifling the healthy structure I so deeply craved. It was as if I had unknowingly handed him the keys to my inner temple, allowing his energy to overpower my own sacred needs and aspirations. But then, the universe, in its infinite wisdom, intervened. It gently nudged us toward separate spaces, and with this shift, I was enveloped in a wave of liberation.

In this newfound sanctuary, I was free—free to craft a life rhythm that resonated with my soul, one that allowed the seeds of healthy habits to blossom. I welcomed the dawn with open arms, taking early morning walks in the embrace of nature, where the stillness and serenity of the first light brought me peace. Slowly, I nurtured a consistent meditation practice, where 20 minutes of stillness became a wellspring of clarity and solace.

Even the act of cooking, which had once been steeped in the toxicity of our shared energy, transformed into a sacred ritual of self-love. As I prepared each nutritious meal with intention, it became a gesture of care, a testament to my journey of healing and self-appreciation. Every bite was a reminder of the goddess within me, the one who was reclaiming her power and nurturing her body with love.

Through these sacred self-care rituals, I rekindled the flame of love and appreciation within myself. I began to honor the goddess I had always been—celebrating my growth, resilience, and transformation. In doing so, I created a life rooted in harmony, balance, and divine love, a life where the goddess within could thrive in her fullest expression.

Tender Love Support, always, Tanisha Duke-Scorza

INSTRUCTIONS

Habit Activities:

As the divine goddess you are, this ritual invites you to explore the sacred terrain of your daily habits, to uncover those that no longer serve your highest self, and to consciously create new ones aligned with your radiant essence. This is a journey of profound self-awareness, where you will gently unveil the patterns that keep you tethered to old energies and open yourself to the habits that nurture your evolution.

I am a goddess, strong, wise, and full of grace

Unveling CURRENT HABITS

Beloved Goddess, you are a sacred being of light, and your journey toward radical self-love calls for the release of anything that no longer serves your highest good. In this ritual, we will gently and powerfully uncover the habits that keep you from fully embracing your divine essence. These habits, though once protective, now dim your radiance, and it is time to lovingly release them.

Sacred Reflection

Find a quiet, serene space where you feel safe to dive deep into your soul. Light a candle or surround yourself with objects that connect you to your divine feminine energy. Take a few deep breaths, grounding yourself in this sacred moment.

Now, ask yourself:

- What habits or patterns are keeping me from fully embodying my goddess nature?

Write down three habits that you feel ready to release. Be honest with yourself, knowing that this is a space of love, not judgment.

Understanding the Root

For each habit, ask yourself:

- What need does this habit attempt to fulfill?
- When did this pattern begin in my life?
- What feelings arise when I engage in this habit?

Allow yourself to dive into the roots of these habits, as they often carry deep emotional or spiritual meaning. Honor the wisdom they've offered, knowing that even unhelpful habits were once coping mechanisms or forms of protection.

Habit 1:_____

Habit 2: _____

Habit 3: _____

---

1. This habit attempt to fulfill_____ it began, _____ and I feel, _____when I engage in this habit.
2. This habit attempt to fulfill_____ it began, _____ and I feel, _____when I engage in this habit.
3. This habit attempt to fulfill_____ it began, _____ and I feel, _____when I engage in this habit.

Creating A HABIT PLAN

A habit plan, in the sacred dance of your goddess journey, is about weaving new rituals into the fabric of your existing divine practices. By aligning a fresh habit with one already cherished, you honor the flow of your daily rhythm. Celebrate each completion with a reward that resonates with your soul, as every small victory nourishes your higher self and reinforces the sacredness of your evolving path.

1: CONNECT YOUR NEW HABIT WITH AN EXISTING ONE

After (old habit), I will (new habit)

2: REWARD

When you link an old habit with a new one, remember to reward yourself. Rewards should not contradict your new habit like eating a bar of chocolate if your new habit is eating a healthy meal.

After (New habit), I will (Reward)

Example

After my nightly routine, I will channel my gratitude onto the pages of my sacred journal. Following this ritual of reflection, I shall indulge in an episode of my beloved series, allowing the joy to wash over me as a reward for honoring my divine practice.

in the space below, create your own habit plan for a new habit you want to implement into your life. In addition, I invite you to use one of the habit trackers sheets located at the back of this sacred text.

Step 1: Connect an old habit to a new one

After _____

I will _____

Step 2: Link your new habit with a reward

After _____

I will _____

Divine Forgiveness and Gratitude

Write a short letter to each habit. In this letter, thank it for what it has taught you, and offer it forgiveness. For example:

"Dear [habit], I see you. I know you were created in a time when I needed you to feel safe, but now, I release you with love and gratitude. I forgive you and myself for any harm caused. I am ready to let go and reclaim my divine power."

By expressing gratitude, you honor the lessons and experiences tied to the habit, allowing you to release it with grace.

_____
_____
_____
_____
_____
_____
_____
_____
_____
_____
_____
_____
_____
_____
_____
_____
_____
_____
_____

Reflection 5:
Setting Boundaries

"Where I heal myself I heal my lineage I am worthy of a peaceful life." unknown

Embarking on my journey of self-love, I faced the formidable challenge of discerning where and how to establish boundaries. The concern for others' perceptions, particularly my family's, loomed large, often leading to boundaries being disregarded and my sense of self eroded. Lost and disheartened, I sought solace in therapy, hoping to gain clarity on boundary-setting.

In just one transformative session, it dawned upon me that the efficacy of my boundaries was undermined by my own actions—I allowed them to be crossed. Unknowingly, I assumed the role of both enforcer and enabler within my familial dynamics, perpetuating a cycle of toxicity that failed to honor my essence and sacred space.

In my quest for self-discovery and healing, I delved deep within, seeking the areas where I needed to erect protective boundaries. It became evident that my 22-year marriage had become a source of trauma; my husband's disregard for my physical and emotional well-being had infused me with negativity. Despite my love for him, I realized the imperative of loving myself above all else. I held onto the belief that our union was destined to transcend generational hardships, yet the misalignment of our paths became starkly apparent.

I vividly recall the moment of epiphany when my youngest child, at the tender age of four, approached me with a poignant question: "Mommy, can you and daddy end this relationship?" With tears welling up in my eyes, I affirmed, "Yes, my dear, we can." It was a watershed moment, a realization that enforcing my boundaries was not just about my well-being but also about setting an example for my child on how to navigate toxic relationships.

Two years have passed since then, and my husband and I now reside in separate homes. Despite our parting, he remains a devoted father, and it was only natural for him to assume primary custody of our children. This journey has been a testament to the power of self-love and the courage to stand firm in protecting one's boundaries, especially in the presence of little ones who look up to us for guidance and resilience.

Tender Love Support, always, Tanisha Duke-Scorza

INSTRUCTIONS

Boundary Activity:

As a goddess of your own journey, you are called to recognize the sacred balance between setting boundaries and surrendering to the divine flow of life. The following activities will guide you to unveil the areas in your world where boundaries are not only necessary but empowering. You will also be invited to release the grip of control, dissolve the illusions of fantasy and idealism, and instead, co-create a vision rooted in truth, freedom, and divine alignment. Step into your power and honor the boundaries that protect your peace, while allowing the universe to guide what is meant to unfold.

My voice is powerful, and I speak my truth with clarity.

My Boundary TRAITS

There exist various types of boundaries, each radiating its unique essence. While we may embody a blend of these boundaries, or shift our limits depending on our surroundings, there lies within each of us a dominant boundary type that guides our interactions and protects our sacred space.

Rigid

- As a goddess, you may guard your sacred heart, choosing not to share your personal feelings or opinions openly.
- You may keep your circle small, protecting your energy and spirit.
- You hold others at a distance, not out of coldness, but as a way to shield your divine essence from potential rejection.
- Your emotions, while powerful, are not always on display, as you carefully guard the sanctity of your inner world.
- Seeking help might be a challenge, for you stand strong in your independence, but remember, even a goddess can gracefully accept support when needed.

Porous

- As a goddess, you must be mindful of your sacred boundaries.
- Resist the urge to over-share, for your thoughts and feelings are treasures to be revealed with care.
- Be cautious not to give away too much of your essence or take on more than you should.
- Guard against becoming overly entangled in the problems of others, and never allow yourself to accept disrespect or abuse.
- Stand firm in your divinity, independent of the approval of others.
- Let your warmth and compassion flow, but never at the expense of your own divine energy.

Healthy

- Stand tall and assertive, dear goddess, with the clarity of your desires and needs.
- Honor your voice and the wisdom of your own opinions.
- Embrace the power in the word "no," whether spoken by you or to you, knowing it too is sacred.
- Share your truths with discernment, choosing who and what to reveal.
- Walk with empathy, holding space for both yourself and others, while respecting the divine rights of all.
- Engage in the dance of life, where negotiation and compromise are your graceful steps.

My Boundary TRAITS

MY BOUNDARY TYPE IS:

Notes.

HOW CAN I IMPROVE ON MY BOUNDARIES?

_____
_____
_____
_____
_____
_____
_____
_____
_____
_____
_____
_____
_____
_____
_____
_____
_____
_____
_____
_____
_____
_____
_____

Reflection 6: Deep Reflection

"Every night before bed I take a minute to feel grateful for everyone & everything in my life."
unknown

In the gentle embrace of retrospection, I find myself immersed in the tapestry of 25 years—a tapestry woven with pivotal moments of growth and the shimmering opportunities that illuminated my roles as a wife and mother. Each moment, each choice, became a beacon guiding me towards the essence of my being—a journey nurtured by introspection, resilience, and unwavering love.

My voyage into the realm of matrimony and motherhood was marked by a thirst for knowledge, a yearning to understand the intricacies of these sacred roles. Growing up in the absence of a two-parent household, I embarked on a quest for wisdom, seeking solace within the pages of books that unraveled the art of being a devoted wife. Christian-based family books became my companions, infusing my beliefs with the sanctity of family values rooted in spirituality.

Amidst my exploration, the voice of Dr. Laura Schlessinger resonated deeply within me—a guiding light advocating for the sanctity of marriage and the valor of stay-at-home mothers. Her words echoed in the corridors of my mind as I navigated the gentle rhythms of nurturing a child and supporting my husband in his noble military endeavors. These were the moments of cultivation, where seeds of dedication and commitment were sown, blossoming into the roles I cherished.

Yet, amidst the ebbs and flows of life, I encountered pivotal junctures—moments where choices bore the weight of transformation. It is these choices that sculpted the path I tread today—a 45-year-old woman, once immersed in the harmonies of family life, now embracing the serenity of solitude. Through myriad life paths and fleeting moments, I have traversed realms of self-discovery, realizing that the path I walk now has liberated me from the cyclical patterns of the past.

This journey has been a testament to the power of introspection and the resilience woven into the fabric of my being. It is the nourishment of mind, body, and spirit—the books I immersed myself in, the wisdom I absorbed, and the beliefs I nurtured—that shaped the essence of who I am today. This reflection is not just a testament to my past but a celebration of the choices, the growth, and the radiant self-love that continue to illuminate my path forward.

Tender Love Support, always, Tanisha Duke-Scorza

INSTRUCTIONS

Deep Reflection Activities:

As the divine goddess you are, this sacred activity calls you to descend into the deepest chambers of your soul, where your truths, triggers, beliefs, and accomplishments reside. In this space of quiet reflection, you will confront the mirrors of your inner world, unveiling what lies beneath your emotions, and gently bringing them into the light of your awareness. This is a journey of courage and love, as you honor all aspects of yourself.

Write down your reflections—your triggers, your beliefs, and your accomplishments. Let each insight guide you toward deeper self-understanding and transformation. As you write, you are weaving together the threads of your soul's tapestry, honoring every piece of your journey with love. This is your moment, goddess, to witness the wholeness of who you are—your shadows and your light, your challenges and your triumphs. In this sacred reflection, you reclaim your power, embodying the fullness of your divine self.

I release any guilt or shame that no longer serves me.

Recognize YOUR TRIGGERS

Recognize that our insecurity triggers can be negative and harmful, but now that you're aware of them, it's time to shower yourself with an empowering love letter that affirms your worth and belief in yourself.

Use the space below to write your letter. Start your letter with "I'm writing because..." and express your deep admiration for yourself with phrases like "I love you because..." and "I appreciate you because..." Reflect on moments when you shined brilliantly and acknowledge your successes and beauty with phrases like "Remember how amazing you were when..." and "You are successful because..." Embrace your uniqueness and perfection with affirmations like "You are uniquely perfect because..." and express gratitude to yourself with "I'm thankful to you because..."

Finally, share your aspirations and wishes for yourself with "What I wish for you is..." and express excitement for your journey ahead with "I am excited for..." Let your words flow from the depths of your divine essence, celebrating the goddess within you.

Notes.

Reflect on YOUR BELIEFS

Delve deep within and awaken the goddess that resides in your soul. Reflect on the moments when your self-love and confidence are tested. Turn your gaze inward to examine the beliefs that shape your existence. Are these beliefs in harmony with your true essence? Do they allow you to shine as your most authentic self? If they fall short, consider what beliefs would genuinely resonate with the divine being you are. Let your intuition, the sacred whisper of your inner goddess, guide you as you identify and embrace the beliefs that align with your highest self.

Celebrate YOUR ACCOMPLISHMENTS

Pause for a moment to honor the magnificence of your journey. Reflect on every achievement, whether grand or humble, and capture them in a list that glows with your radiant energy and pride. Write down all that fills your heart with joy and pride, recognizing the strength, resilience, and grace that has guided you. Hold this list sacred, and revisit it whenever you need a gentle reminder of your boundless potential and limitless capability. Let the brilliance of your accomplishments uplift and empower you as you continue to walk the path of radical self-love and divine empowerment.

Notes.

Mental Health Break:

Reflection:
How do you feel? What shifts have you noticed within your mind, body, and soul? Acknowledge any reflections or emotions that surface as you continue your journey of radical self-love. Embrace this sacred process, by journaling, doodling or drawing.

Grab a cup of tea and let your mind be free!

Reflection 7:
Engaging in positive self-talk

I forgive & release to allow for my own healing." unknown

This is by far the most important chapter in this book.
This is where the magic happens.
Think about you, who is talking to you?
As a divine goddess, your words are sacred—they hold the power to shape your reality. What you say to yourself becomes the foundation of your existence, for your inner dialogue is a reflection of the light that resides within you. In every quiet moment of contemplation, you have the opportunity to rewrite your story, one thought at a time.
In these still moments, when we confront the whispers of our soul, we often face the question: "Am I my worst enemy?" This question is not meant to diminish you, but to invite you into a deeper understanding of how your self-talk can either uplift or dim your divine radiance. For years, I, too, wrapped myself in the roles I believed defined happiness, yet beneath it all, there was a quiet discord—a part of me yearning for true alignment with my essence.
It was a single, honest reflection from my daughter that shattered the illusion I had crafted: "Mommy, look at you. You ain't happy!" Those words revealed what I had hidden from myself. It was a moment of reckoning, standing before the mirror, realizing that my self-talk had been masking my deepest desires with toxic positivity. I had been silencing my true voice.
But in that moment of realization, I found empowerment. I understood that the way I spoke to myself would become the reality I lived. As I began to shift my internal dialogue, I saw the profound change it brought—not just to my own life, but to the way I engaged with the world around me.
This is your invitation, goddess, to engage in positive self-talk that aligns with your divine truth. Peel back the layers of societal expectations, release the limitations you've inherited, and embrace the sacredness of speaking to yourself with love, compassion, and honesty. The words you choose are your power.

Tender Love Support, always, Tanisha Duke-Scorza

INSTRUCTIONS

Positive Self Talk Activities:

Beloved Goddess, your words carry the power to heal, transform, and uplift. As we navigate life's trials, we often forge shields—protective patterns that help us survive yet can also distance us from our true selves. These defense shields are crafted from our need to shield ourselves from pain, and while they have served their purpose, it is time to gently set them down and embrace the nurturing power of positive self-talk.

In this sacred activity, you will reflect on the self-protective patterns that have shaped your life, while shifting your inner dialogue to one that reflects your divine worth. Positive self-talk is your tool for dismantling the shields that no longer serve you and inviting in the essence of goddess within.

I choose joy, peace, and freedom every day.

the Power OF WORDS
the Divine Power of Words: Spelling as a Sacred Spell:

Beloved Goddess, as we embark on this journey of exploring our self-talk, let us delve into the mystical influence of words, a profound spell-crafting that shapes our reality. Dr. Masaru Emoto, a revered scientist, unveiled the enchanting power of words through his experiments. He discovered that the molecular structure of water transforms dramatically when exposed to different words. Harmful words disfigured the water's structure, while words of love, prayer, and gratitude conjured beautiful, intricate crystals.

Dr. Emoto's findings illuminate words, as being sound vibrations, holding the power to affect and influence us and everything around us. As beings of frequency, the energy we emit, especially through spoken words, alters our environment. Words are the sacred tools through which this energy is conveyed.

Reflect on this: our bodies are composed of nearly 70% water. Consider the impact of negative thoughts, statements, or conversations on us if words can so profoundly affect water and other living elements like food and plants.

Each word carries potent energy, capable of invoking a spectrum of emotions. Words charged with negativity can evoke feelings tied to past wounds, instantly altering our emotional state. Recall moments when harsh criticism or mockery shifted your feelings dramatically—such is the power of words.

Therefore, dear Goddess, be mindful of your words, for they wield immense power. Choose them with care, as they shape not only your world but the worlds of those around you. Embrace the sacred art of spelling, and let your words be a source of light and love.

Understanding MY DEFENSE SHIELDS

Our defense shields are the resilient armor we forge in response to life's trials, crafted to shield us from trauma's harsh blows. They emerge as our protective fortresses, our instinctive responses to safeguard our well-being.

As you embark on this introspective journey, consider which of these 11 self-protective patterns resonate within your being. Embrace honesty as your guiding light, for it is in acknowledging these shields that we begin to unravel the layers of our souls and embark on the path to profound self-awareness and healing

- [ ] Being a people pleaser - Yes woman
- [ ] Being Controlling - guilting or manipulating others
- [ ] Displaying superiority - Trying to be perfect/ better than
- [ ] Settling - Something is better than nothing
- [ ] Pessimistic - Suspicious and negative
- [ ] Ignoring your intuition - letting your ego not soul guide you
- [ ] Using addictions as a crutch - Alcohol, sex, shopping etc.
- [ ] Delaying tactics - Procrastination,
- [ ] Being a fixer - Staying in toxic relationships
- [ ] Seeking validation - not feeling good enough
- [ ] Creating drama - feeling safe in chaos

Understanding My Defense Shields *Cont.*

Reflect upon the tapestry of your childhood and life experiences with the gentle wisdom of acknowledging your self-talk.

Notes.

Where do you think each of these defensive shield's stem from?

LOOKING INSIDE
Part 1

As a goddess, you stand as the embodiment of grace, harmony, and inner power. This activity invites you to pause and reflect on whether your inner dialogue truly reflects the divinity you carry within. Ask yourself:

- **Does my inner dialogue echo my highest values and sacred principles?**
- **Do I treat myself with the kindness, respect, and empathy I deserve as a divine being?**
- **What sacred steps can I take to further cultivate this inner harmony and balance within my soul?**

(These reflective questions are the seeds of self-love, guiding you to align your self-talk with your divine essence.)

REFLECTING ON YOUR SACRED RELATIONSHIP WITH SELF

Begin this journey by listing the loving actions you have taken for yourself within the last 24 hours.

Your list might include acts such as:

I brewed myself a cup of herbal tea.
I embraced and shared warm hugs from loved ones.
I took part in a sacred bath, dressed in an herbal satchel.

These examples are tangible expressions of self-love, acts of grace that you have bestowed upon yourself. Often, we rush through our days, overlooking these divine gestures, as if they were insignificant. But are they?

Each act of kindness you offer to yourself is a sacred ritual, a testament to your divine worth. It is time to honor these blessings, recognizing that the world owes us nothing—yet, we owe ourselves everything.

Use the space on the following page to document your acts of self-love, your sacred interactions with yourself. Let this list be a testament to your journey toward deeper self-awareness and divine balance.

Reflection Part 1

HOW DOES MY SELF-TALK ALIGN WITH THE GODDESS WITHIN ME?

Notes.

LOOKING INSIDE
Part 2

Am I, in all my divine essence, extending to myself the boundless kindness, respect, and empathy that I so freely offer to the world? As you journey inward and reflect, ask yourself: Am I embodying the sacred energies of love and compassion toward myself? In the stillness of your introspection, balance emerges. It is here that you can truly measure the give and take, the ebb and flow, within your relationships, be it with another soul or the vast universe itself—whether in the fleeting moments of a day or across the tapestry of a decade.

Often, we traverse life with an unspoken sense of entitlement, questioning, "Why was I not chosen?" or "Why did I not receive?" or "Why does my beloved not see my worth?" These thoughts spring from the illusion that the world owes us something, leading to frustration when our desires go unmet, reinforcing the idea that others are responsible for our happiness.

Now, embrace this divine truth: Is life more abundant when we clutch at what we believe is ours, or when we devote ourselves to the sacred act of giving, of pouring forth our love and light? The true essence of self-love flourishes not in seeking to be served, but in serving others, in being the embodiment of love itself.

For the next ten minutes, engage in a sacred ritual. Chronicle the gifts of your spirit you have shared with others in the past 24 hours. Perhaps you contributed to a worthy cause, prepared a meal infused with love, sent a heartfelt message to a friend, or offered a genuine compliment. Be specific in your recollections, avoiding broad generalities like "I was kind" or "I was supportive." Delve deep into your actions and the ripples they created.

View this as a sacred journey of self-awareness. Have you been consistent in your offerings of love? If you recall sharing a smile, have you also received the smiles bestowed upon you with grace? This practice is not merely about tallying deeds but about recognizing the divine exchange of energy in your life.

Reflection Part 2

Notes

AM I TREATING MYSELF WITH KINDNESS, RESPECT, AND EMPATHY?

LOOKING INSIDE
Part 3

What sacred steps can I take to cultivate inner harmony and balance within my divine life? While it may seem challenging, this question holds profound importance in truly understanding our authentic selves and embracing the divine dignity we possess. We often notice how others might disrupt our peace—a brief, unintentional bump, a delay in the grocery line—but do we turn that same perceptive eye inward? Do we extend the same awareness to our own actions, acknowledging how we may contribute to such disturbances? The path to divine growth lies in this deep self-reflection.

I invite you to set aside ten minutes to reflect deeply on moments when your words or actions may have caused discomfort or difficulty to others in the past day. Did you speak with harshness when gentleness was needed? Did you leave tasks unfinished, expecting others to carry your burden? Were you inattentive to a friend's heartful message? Pinpoint these occurrences with the clarity of a goddess, seeing them for what they truly are.

Upon completing these reflections, take a pause to review your list. Did any insights or realizations bring forth a divine "aha moment"? What newfound wisdom has emerged from your reflections? Contemplate the blessings you may have taken for granted and the changes you can lovingly embrace moving forward. Whom do you need to honor more in your life, including the sacred self that resides within you? Remember, the energy of our thoughts and intentions is powerful and expansive. By nurturing positivity and self-love in your internal dialogue, you not only become a radiant beacon of love for others but also cultivate a deeper well of love and compassion within yourself. In this way, your divine essence aligns with the universal harmony, creating a life of balance, peace, and profound inner beauty.

Reflection

Part 3

WHAT STEPS CAN I TAKE TO CULTIVATE INNER HARMONY AND BALANCE IN MY LIFE?

Notes.

Reflection 8:
Divine Self Care

Beloved, practicing self-care is often misunderstood, shrouded in layers of external validations and fleeting comforts. We've been conditioned to believe that a manicure, a vacation, or lounging by the poolside with a captivating book are the pinnacles of self-care. Do not mistake me—I too relish the serene moments spent poolside with a book, a sanctuary away from the world. Yet, in my journey to uncover the deepest layers of my authentic self, I recognized a profound truth: true self-care requires a deeper, more radical approach, one that transcends the surface and penetrates the soul.

In my sacred quest for self-discovery, I knew that I must be intentional about redefining what it means to care for myself. It is not merely in the indulgences, but in the profound act of nurturing my soul. I embarked on an inward journey, delving into the depths of my being through the ancient practices of meditation, yoga, and journaling. These were not just routines but sacred rituals, portals that opened my heart to the universe's infinite love. Through conversations with the wise and the open-hearted, I began to feel the energy that connects us all.

I challenged myself, dearest, to embrace love in its purest forms, to be open to receiving love in ways I had never considered. Through this exploration, I uncovered a divine revelation: my true love language is consistency. It is in the daily acts of showing up for myself, in the unwavering commitment to my well-being, that I found the essence of self-love.

On the days when the shadows of my past neglect would creep into my consciousness, I did not turn away. Instead, I invited them in, giving myself the grace to acknowledge my pain, to feel it, and to understand where I needed to forgive myself. In this sacred space, I found healing.

You, too, are worthy of this grace. As you walk this path, remember that self-care is not just an act; it is a way of being. It is in how you speak to yourself, how you nourish your body, and how you honor your spirit. It is in the love you give to others and the love you allow yourself to receive. It is the delicate balance of giving and receiving, of action and reflection, of strength and vulnerability.

May you, like the goddess you are, hold yourself in the highest esteem, and may your self-care be a reflection of the divine love within you.

Tender Love Support, always, Tanisha Scorza

INSTRUCTIONS

Self-Care Activities

Beloved, this is your sacred moment to gather the treasures you need, to ritualize your self-care, and to step fully into the goddess you are destined to be. Trust the journey, for you are divinely guided and deeply loved.

I choose to see myself through the eyes of love.

Looking at SELF-CARE

What is missing, dear one? What sacred elements must you gather to journey from where you stand now to the destined place that calls you? Consider both the tangible and intangible treasures you seek. What will you need to summon within yourself mentally, physically, emotionally, and intellectually to bridge this sacred distance? What divine challenges stand before you, waiting to be gracefully overcome? Use the space below to jot down whatever comes to mind.

Notes.

EMBRACE YOUR DIVINE ESSENCE
WITH
EMBODIMENT RITUALS

Honor Your Temple with Plant Nourishment: Dedicate sacred days to feed your body with the pure essence of the Earth, free from meat and dairy. Let your spirit rise as you nourish yourself with nature's gifts.

Awaken the Goddess Within Through Movement: Celebrate the strength and grace of your divine vessel by engaging in physical rituals. Allow your body to move in ways that honor your inner power and vitality.

Embrace the Sacred Art of Intimacy: Open your heart to the warmth of affection and connection. Be present in the sacred dance of intimacy, cherishing the moments of closeness that nourish your soul.

Safeguard Your Divine Health: Regularly commune with healers to ensure the well-being of your earthly form. These check-ups are a sacred duty to the goddess within, ensuring your body remains a vessel of strength and vitality.

Surrender to the Rhythm of Rest: Gift yourself the blessing of 8 hours of deep, restorative sleep each night. In this sacred time, your body, mind, and spirit rejuvenate, preparing you to rise anew with each dawn.

Connect with Gaia's Essence: Spend 15 minutes each day in nature, absorbing the wisdom and energy of the Earth. Let the whispers of the wind and the embrace of the sun remind you of your connection to all that is.

Honor the Sabbath of Your Soul: Take days away from work to rest, reflect, and reconnect with your true essence. These moments of pause are sacred, allowing you to return to your duties with renewed vigor.

Release the Bonds of Technology: Detox from the digital world to reclaim your mind, body, and spirit. Disconnect to reconnect with the divine flow within you.

Stretch Your Body to Expand Your Spirit: Engage in the sacred practice of stretching, lengthening your muscles as you expand your inner space. Let this ritual open channels of energy throughout your being.

Bath in the Healing Waters: Immerse yourself in an Epsom salt bath, allowing the waters to cleanse and rejuvenate your divine form. As the salts dissolve, so too do the stresses and tensions, leaving you purified and whole.

EMBRACE YOUR DIVINE ESSENCE WITH SPIRITUAL RITUALS

Explore the Depths of Your Inner Landscape: Engage in divine inquiry through discovery questions, inviting wisdom and clarity to guide your path. Allow coaching or therapy to be sacred space where you unearth the truths that have long been buried within.

Channel Your Divine Essence Through the Written Word: Embrace the sacred art of journaling. Let your thoughts, emotions, and revelations flow freely onto the pages, capturing the essence of your journey.

Map Your Path with Celestial Tools: Utilize workbooks and planners as your sacred scrolls, guiding your steps with intention and purpose. Let these tools help you manifest your divine vision in the material world.

Invoke the Power of the Earth: Use essential oils as an anointing ritual, allowing their sacred aromas to elevate your spirit, calm your mind, and balance your energies.

Gaze Upon the Goddess Within: Practice mirror work, looking into your own eyes and speaking words of love, affirmation, and truth. See the reflection of the divine goddess that resides within you.

Unite with Your Sacred Circle: Find your tribe, a support group of like-minded souls who resonate with your divine frequency. Together, you can uplift and empower each other on your spiritual journeys.

Express the Goddess Through Creativity: Engage in drawing or painting as a divine practice, letting your creativity flow freely and giving form to the visions within your soul.

Breathe Life into Your Spirit: Incorporate short breathing exercises into your daily rituals, allowing the breath of life to fill your lungs and rejuvenate your being. Let each breath be a reminder of your divine essence.

EMBRACE YOUR DIVINE ESSENCE WITH NURTURING RITUALS

Honor Your Temple with Plant Nourishment: Dedicate sacred days to feed your body with the pure essence of the Earth, free from meat and dairy. Let your spirit rise as you nourish yourself with nature's gifts.

Awaken the Goddess Within Through Movement: Celebrate the strength and grace of your divine vessel by engaging in physical rituals. Allow your body to move in ways that honor your inner power and vitality.

Embrace the Sacred Art of Intimacy: Open your heart to the warmth of affection and connection. Be present in the sacred dance of intimacy, cherishing the moments of closeness that nourish your soul.

Safeguard Your Divine Health: Regularly commune with healers to ensure the well-being of your earthly form. These check-ups are a sacred duty to the goddess within, ensuring your body remains a vessel of strength and vitality.

Surrender to the Rhythm of Rest: Gift yourself the blessing of 8 hours of deep, restorative sleep each night. In this sacred time, your body, mind, and spirit rejuvenate, preparing you to rise anew with each dawn.

Connect with Gaia's Essence: Spend 15 minutes each day in nature, absorbing the wisdom and energy of the Earth. Let the whispers of the wind and the embrace of the sun remind you of your connection to all that is.

Honor the Sabbath of Your Soul: Take days away from work to rest, reflect, and reconnect with your true essence. These moments of pause are sacred, allowing you to return to your duties with renewed vigor.

Release the Bonds of Technology: Detox from the digital world to reclaim your mind, body, and spirit. Disconnect to reconnect with the divine flow within you.

Stretch Your Body to Expand Your Spirit: Engage in the sacred practice of stretching, lengthening your muscles as you expand your inner space. Let this ritual open channel of energy throughout your being.

Bathe in the Healing Waters: Immerse yourself in an Epsom salt bath, allowing the waters to cleanse and rejuvenate your divine form. As the salts dissolve, so too do the stresses and tensions, leaving you purified and whole.

EMBRACE YOUR DIVINE ESSENCE WITH SACRED RITUALS

Communion with the Source: Engage in prayer or speak to the Divine Source, allowing your spirit to connect with the infinite energy that sustains all of creation. Let your words be offerings of love, gratitude, and guidance as you align with the cosmic flow.

Ground Your Spirit in Nature: Reconnect with the Earth by grounding yourself in nature. Feel the sacred energy of the soil beneath your feet, anchoring your soul to the heartbeat of the Mother Goddess herself.

Embrace the Healing Waters: Surround yourself with the calming presence of water—whether by a tranquil lake, a flowing river, or the vast ocean. Water purifies and rejuvenates, washing away what no longer serves you and restoring your inner harmony.

Witness the Divine Dance of the Sun: Watch the sun rise and set, witnessing the daily miracle of light. Let these moments be your reminder of the cycles of life, the eternal dance between light and dark, and the beauty of each new beginning.

Journey Within through Meditation: Meditate to find stillness within, where the voice of the goddess whispers truths and wisdom. In this sacred silence, your inner light shines brightest, illuminating the path of your soul.

Move with Divine Grace: Dance or practice yoga, celebrating the divine energy flowing through your body. With each movement, you honor the sacred temple of your being, expressing your connection to the universal rhythms of life.

Harmonize with Celestial Frequencies: Listen to the healing frequency of 432 Hz, attuning your spirit to the harmonious vibrations of the universe. Let these sounds elevate your consciousness, bringing peace and balance to your soul.

Revitalize with Crystal Energy: Take breaks to engage with your crystals, allowing their unique energies to cleanse and empower you. These gems are earth's sacred gifts, tools to amplify your intentions and connect you to higher realms.

Purify Your Sacred Space: Use sage to cleanse your environment, sweeping away negative energies and inviting divine protection and light into your space. This ancient ritual purifies the air and sanctifies your surroundings.

Nourish Your Soul with Wisdom: Read spiritual books, feeding your mind and spirit with the wisdom of the ages. These sacred texts guide you on your journey, offering insights and revelations that align you with your highest self.

EMBRACE YOUR DIVINE ESSENCE TO TRANSFORMATION RITUALS

Collaborate with a Spiritual Guide: Seek the wisdom of a coach or mentor, one who embodies the divine qualities you aspire to cultivate. Allow their guidance to illuminate your path as you journey toward your highest self.

Adorn Yourself with Role Models: Find a role model whose essence resonates with your soul's aspirations. Let their life be a beacon of inspiration, showing you what is possible when you align with your divine purpose.

Craft Sacred Intentions with SMART Goals: Write down your SMART goals—specific, measurable, attainable, relevant, and time bound. These goals are the sacred blueprints of your desires, the steps that will guide you closer to your divine destiny.

Awaken the Goddess Within through Self-Awareness: Focus on deepening your self-awareness, peeling back the layers of your being to reveal the goddess within. In this state of heightened awareness, you discover the truth of who you are and who you are meant to become.

Weave a Vision Board of Dreams: Create a vision board that reflects your highest aspirations, a tangible representation of your soul's deepest desires. Each image, word, and symbol are a prayer, manifesting the life you are destined to live.

Expand Your Sacred Circle: Meet new people, inviting fresh energies and perspectives into your life. Each new connection is a thread in the divine tapestry of your existence, enriching your journey with wisdom and love.

Cherish the Sacred Bonds of Family: Spend time with family, honoring the sacred bonds that connect you to your lineage. In their presence, you find grounding and a deeper understanding of your place in the cosmic order.

Engage in a Sacred SWOT Analysis: Conduct a personal SWOT analysis—assessing your strengths, weaknesses, opportunities, and threats. This exercise is a sacred act of self-reflection, empowering you to align more closely with your divine purpose.

Rebirth Yourself as the Radiant Goddess You Are: Rebrand yourself, shedding old identities that no longer serve you. Embrace your true essence, emerging anew as the radiant, powerful goddess you were always meant to be.

EMBRACE YOUR DIVINE ESSENCE
TO
BALANCE RITUALS

Seek the Wisdom of a Sacred Mentor: Align yourself with a mentor who embodies the qualities and knowledge you aspire to cultivate. Allow their guidance to illuminate your path, nurturing your growth and elevating your divine potential.

Journey to Rejuvenate Your Spirit: Take time to embark on a sacred vacation, a retreat from the ordinary that allows your soul to rejuvenate. Whether by the sea, in the mountains, or under the stars, let this be a time to reconnect with your inner goddess.

Establish Sacred Boundaries: Set firm boundaries that honor your energy and protect your sacred space. By doing so, you empower yourself to flourish and maintain harmony within your life.

Honor the Sacred Balance of Time: Leave work on time, respecting the divine rhythm of life that calls you to balance labor with rest. Your time is a sacred gift; cherish it.

Delegate with Grace and Wisdom: Trust in the ability of others and delegate tasks as a goddess would, with grace and confidence. By sharing responsibilities, you create space for your own growth and self-care.

Expand Your Divine Knowledge: Enroll in a course that enriches your mind and soul. Education is a sacred journey, one that deepens your wisdom and aligns you with your higher purpose.

Envision and Manifest Your Future: Create a five-year career plan, a divine map that guides you toward your professional aspirations. This plan is your commitment to your growth and the embodiment of your career dreams.

Master Your Divine Craft: Dedicate yourself to mastering an area completely, becoming an expert in your chosen field. In this mastery, you reflect the dedication and excellence of a goddess.

Harmonize Your Sacred Spaces: Cultivate a balance between work and home, ensuring that both realms are places of peace and fulfillment. By creating this harmony, you honor the goddess within, who thrives in environments of love and balance.

Create Your Own

SELF- CARE RITUALS

Create your own self-care rituals in the below wheel. Feel free to use the some of the examples the pages that follows for inspiration.

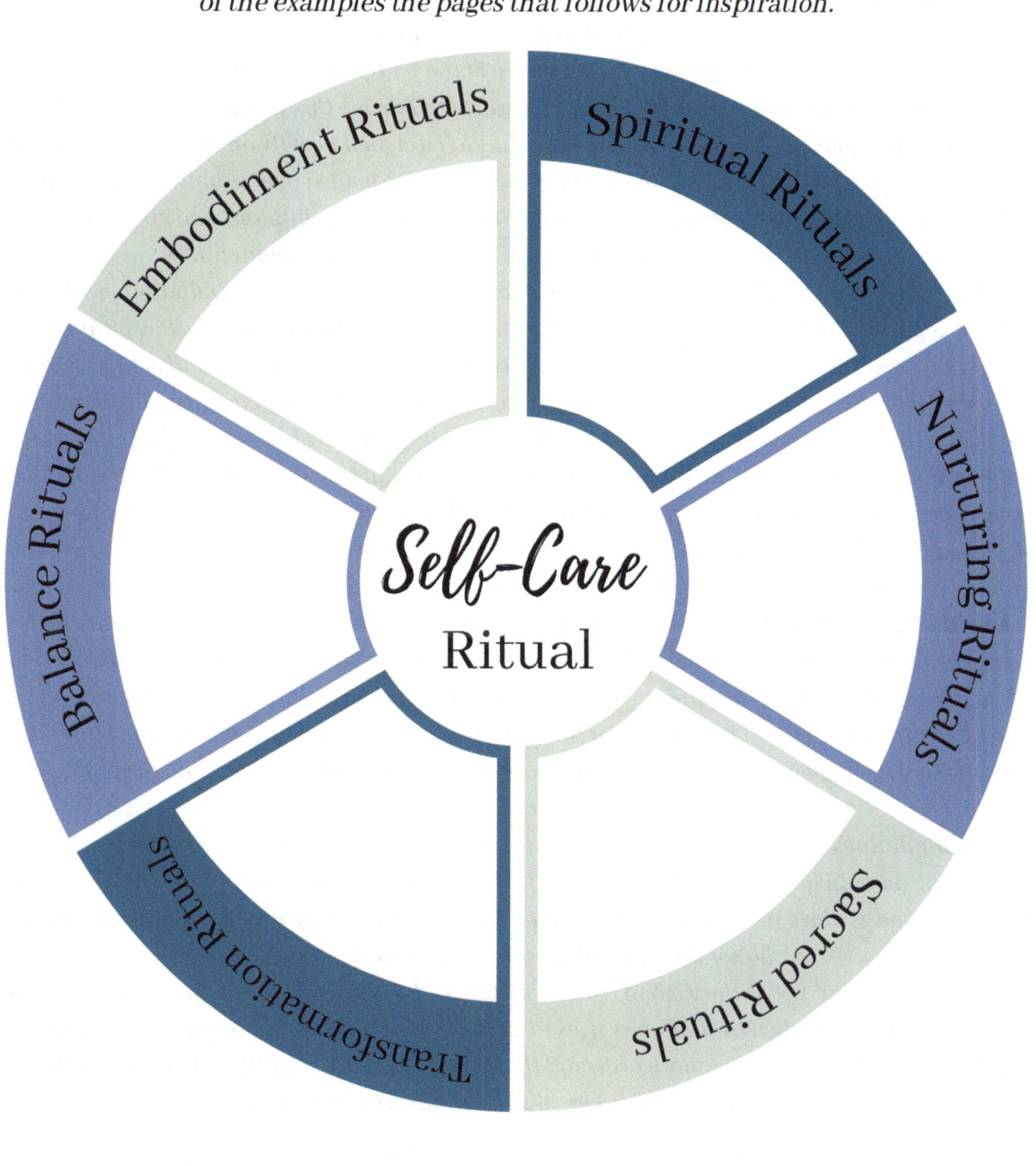

- Embodiment Rituals
- Spiritual Rituals
- Nurturing Rituals
- Sacred Rituals
- Transformation Rituals
- Balance Rituals

Self-Care Ritual

Reflection 9:
Becoming Mindful

"INHALE EXHALE ONE MOMENT AT A TIME." UNKNOWN

For me, mindfulness was a practice long before I ever knew its name. It wasn't something I learned in a quiet meditation room or through guided lessons—it was birthed from the darkest corners of my life, where my spirit was tested beyond measure. It was 2009 when I was no longer known by my name but by a number: X28637. The weight of that moment shattered everything I thought I knew about myself and my world. When the prison door closed behind me, and the life I had known was stripped away in an instant, I became deeply aware of the power of presence.

Facing twelve years for embezzlement felt like the world telling me this was where I was destined to spend my adult life. The embarrassment I brought to myself weighed heavily on my heart, but even then, I knew I was divinely protected. I felt it in the DA's whisper as she leaned over, admitting she didn't want to give me any time at all, but the state required it. They gave me the minimum, and after four years of delays, I was sentenced to two years in California State Penitentiary.

During the 366 days I spent incarcerated, I unknowingly learned the essence of mindfulness. Each day was a test, a practice of being fully present in my own pain, my own accountability. It was there, in the stillness of that confinement, that I began to see clearly how my thoughts, beliefs, and actions had led me to that very place. No longer could I escape my choices or run from the consequences. I had to stand in the truth of what I had done, and in doing so, I was forced to reevaluate what I held sacred.

In those moments of stillness, I realized I had placed value on all the wrong things. I had worshiped money above all else, and it led me to a path of destruction. But there, within those walls, I began to understand that character, wisdom, and integrity are what truly hold value in this life. I learned that if anyone ever questioned my character, I no longer needed to defend myself. I know who I am. I embody both the light and the dark, and while I have danced in the shadows, I always choose the light.

It wasn't until 2015, during my journey to India to meet with the Dalai Lama, that I finally had a name for what I had been practicing: mindfulness. The presence I had embraced during my incarceration was my saving grace. It allowed me to hold myself accountable, to stand in my truth, and to heal. Mindfulness became the tool through which I regained control over my life, over my thoughts, and over the narrative I was creating.

Through mindfulness, I learned to love myself fully—every part of me, the mistakes, the triumphs, the light, and the dark. In loving myself, I was able to truly love others, and I realized that by divine order, you must love me as I love you. We are reflections of one another, and through mindfulness, we learn to honor the light within ourselves and each other.

I stand before you now, not as the woman I once was, but as the goddess I have always been. I choose to live in my light, even when the darkness tries to claim me. Mindfulness has given me the power to choose, the wisdom to know my worth, and the grace to love deeply, fully, and without fear.

Tender Love Support, always, Tanisha Duke-Scorza

INSTRUCTIONS

Mindfulness Activities

Beloved Goddess, the power of mindfulness lies in your ability to honor the present moment with a heart full of gratitude. To practice mindfulness is to surrender fully to the sacred now—a space where your divine essence meets the beauty of existence as it unfolds. Gratitude is the key that unlocks the fullness of this moment, allowing you to see the blessings woven into each breath, each experience, each step of your journey.

In these activities, you will learn to intertwine mindfulness with gratitude, for it is through the recognition of the gifts around and within you that you can fully embrace radical self-love.

Goddess, your journey of mindfulness is a divine unfolding. Gratitude is the doorway through which you enter the present moment, and in the sacred now, you find your true power, your peace, and your love.

I embrace change as a natural part of my growth.

Surrendering to the SCARED NOW

Dearest Goddess,

To dwell in the sacred present is to honor the divine flow of life itself. Shifting your focus away from the past or future liberates your soul and invites you to fully embrace the beauty of now. In this moment, there are no worries, no "what ifs," only the sweet essence of presence. Here, you reclaim your power and breathe deeply into your being.

To embody this practice, choose three daily tasks you engage in as an offering to your divine self. Commit to being fully present in each one, allowing the moment to reveal its magic.

For example, when you sip your tea:
- Feel the warmth of the cup cradled in your hands, like an intimate embrace.
- Inhale the rich aroma, letting it fill your senses, grounding you in this very second.
- As the liquid kisses your lips, notice the tingling sensation and the way it nourishes your body, soul, and spirit.

Write down the sensations, thoughts, and feelings that arise from being fully present in these sacred tasks. Surrender to the moment. Let the beauty of now wash over you, and drink in all it has to offer. Milk the moment, beloved, for it is filled with divine wisdom, ready to nourish your journey of self-love.

TASK:
SENSATIONS / THOUGHTS / FEELINGS:

TASK:
SENSATIONS / THOUGHTS / FEELINGS:

TASK:
SENSATIONS / THOUGHTS / FEELINGS:

Grounding Gratitude Practice

Instructions:

1. Find a quiet space where you can sit comfortably without distractions. Close your eyes, take a few deep breaths, and center yourself.
2. Place one hand on your heart and the other on your abdomen, feeling your breath as it rises and falls. Take five slow, deep breaths. Focus on the present moment and your connection to your body.
3. Gratitude List:
    - On a blank sheet of paper or in your journal, write down three things you are grateful for in this moment. They can be small, like the warmth of the sun or a comforting conversation, or larger, like your health or personal growth.
    - Next, write down three things you love about yourself. They could be personality traits, accomplishments, or aspects of your appearance.
4. Reflection:
    - After you've written your gratitude list, take a moment to reflect on how these things make you feel.
    - How does recognizing your strengths and blessings shift your mindset from negativity to self-love?
5. Affirmation:
    - End the practice by writing or saying this affirmation:

"I am worthy of love, care, and respect. I honor the beauty within me, and I am healing each day."

MIRACLES NATURALLY OCCUR DAILY FOR ME
I AM LIVING IN THE FLOW OF LIFE!

Gratitude PROMPTS

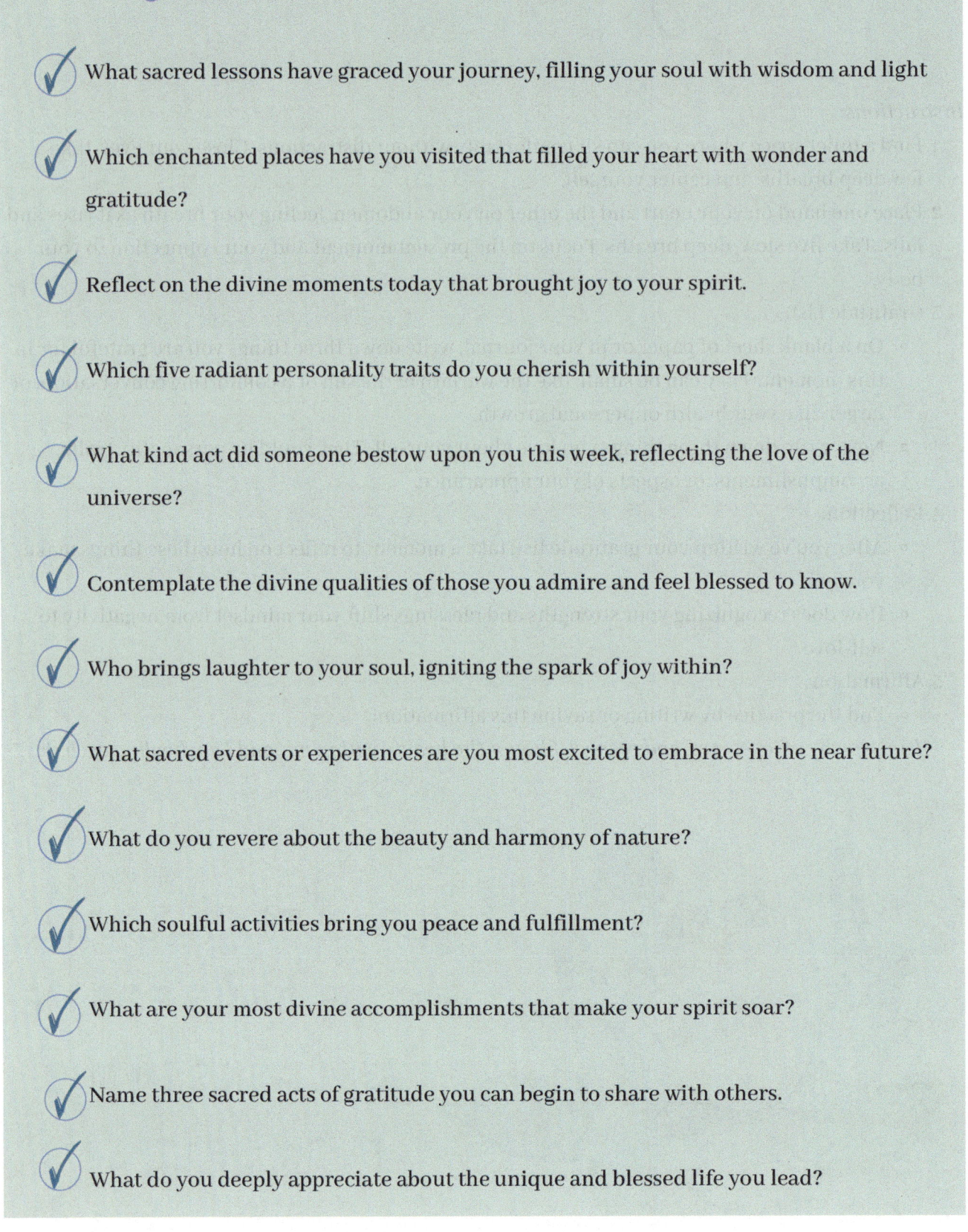

- ✓ What sacred lessons have graced your journey, filling your soul with wisdom and light

- ✓ Which enchanted places have you visited that filled your heart with wonder and gratitude?

- ✓ Reflect on the divine moments today that brought joy to your spirit.

- ✓ Which five radiant personality traits do you cherish within yourself?

- ✓ What kind act did someone bestow upon you this week, reflecting the love of the universe?

- ✓ Contemplate the divine qualities of those you admire and feel blessed to know.

- ✓ Who brings laughter to your soul, igniting the spark of joy within?

- ✓ What sacred events or experiences are you most excited to embrace in the near future?

- ✓ What do you revere about the beauty and harmony of nature?

- ✓ Which soulful activities bring you peace and fulfillment?

- ✓ What are your most divine accomplishments that make your spirit soar?

- ✓ Name three sacred acts of gratitude you can begin to share with others.

- ✓ What do you deeply appreciate about the unique and blessed life you lead?

Feeling GRATEFUL

Each day, I invite you to embrace the power of gratitude by selecting three things that stir your heart with appreciation. In my sacred journey of gratitude, I began with a simple notebook, recording my blessings. Later, I transitioned to a gratitude jar, capturing each cherished moment. Now, I speak my gratitude aloud, at any moment that moves my spirit. I have woven gratitude into the fabric of my being, living in its divine flow. Whenever my thoughts attempt to lead me astray, I pause, acknowledging the path they wish to take, and with gentle compassion, I say, "Not today." I give thanks for the very thing that reminds me of the depth of my gratitude.

Envision ways to immerse yourself fully in the radiant energy of gratitude. Consider how you might weave this sacred practice into the very essence of your being, allowing it to illuminate your thoughts, words, and actions each day.

In what divine ways are you envisioning to immerse yourself in the energy of gratitude?	*Which sacred practices are you choosing to move forward with on this journey?*

Reflection 10: Radical Self-love

"Of course you love me, I love me. But I really hope you love you more than you love me."- Tanisha Duke-Scorza

Radical self-love is the sacred awakening to the divine truth that each morning, you rise enveloped in the purest form of love—a love that emanates from within. This love is steadfast, unwavering, and deeply connected to the very essence of your being. It does not depend on external validation but is rooted in the profound recognition of your own worth, beauty, and power.

In the quiet moments of dawn, as the sun graces the horizon with its first light, I am reminded of the sacred love that dwells within me. This love is a divine gift from the universe, coursing through my veins, affirming my inherent value and the unique beauty of my soul. With every breath, I am reminded of my worthiness, not in the eyes of others, but in the eyes of my own sacred self.

When someone shares that they love you, the goddess within you responds with grace and certainty, "I love me too, and I hope you love yourself even more than you love me." This statement is not just an affirmation of self-love but a blessing, inviting others to embark on their journey toward radical self-acceptance and divine love.

As I move through the world, I carry this love within me, letting it guide my actions and interactions. It is a love that radiates outward, touching everyone I encounter, creating a ripple effect of positivity and light. In this way, I become a beacon of love, a source of healing and comfort for those around me.

The sensation of being loved is sweet, but choosing to radiate love, to become a beacon of love, is truly divine. This experience transcends the ordinary and touches the sublime, drawing you closer to the goddess you are destined to be.

To embody Agape, the highest form of unconditional love, is to live in a state of gratitude, where love flows through you like a river—nourishing, healing, and purifying everything in its path. It is not just a feeling but a choice, a conscious decision to radiate love in every moment, to every being, and in every situation. This divine love is not merely received; it is generated from within and shared freely with the world, creating a ripple effect of love and light.

A goddess who embodies the essence of Agape, radiating unconditional love, is a beacon of divine compassion and boundless affection. She is the purest expression of love, transcending all earthly limitations and embracing every soul with warmth and understanding. Her love is a gentle yet powerful current, flowing freely and endlessly, nourishing all who come into her presence. In her, there is no judgment—only the deep, unwavering embrace of acceptance and kindness. She is a vessel of the highest form of love, a goddess who heals, nurtures, and uplifts the world with her radiant, unconditional heart.

Tender Love Support, always, Tanisha Duke-Scorza

INSTRUCTIONS

Self-Love Activities:

Beloved Goddess, your journey to radical self-love requires sacred commitment, intentional acknowledgment, and powerful affirmations. In this activity, you will engage in three transformative practices: acknowledging your divine worth, creating a self-love contract, and crafting a mantra that honors your essence. Each step will bring you closer to embodying the goddess within.

I am connected to the divine wisdom of the universe.

ACKNOWLEDGGMENT OF *Self-love*

A declaration is your sacred statement of intentions, motives, and radiant brilliance. Whenever you feel your path wavering, let your declaration be the guiding light that helps you refocus and realign with your dream life.

Here my statement of Self Love:

She is a luminous force of ambition and leadership, a divine beacon guiding the path for women who walk in her footsteps. A trailblazer with a soul that seeks to inspire and be inspired, she dedicates her life to uplifting the lives of women, weaving a legacy of transformative change into the fabric of this world. Her honesty, loyalty, and kindness are the very essence of her being, and she thrives in the sacred act of elevating others.

Even in the face of life's storms, she stands resolute, embraced by a circle of kindred spirits who share her divine vision. She understands that the journey to her divine purpose is a sacred pilgrimage, not a fleeting race, and she advances with unyielding determination, knowing her destiny is woven with the threads of a higher calling. No force shall hinder this goddess as she manifests her dreams and empowers other women to rise in their own divine power. She is a rare and precious soul, destined to live the life she has so beautifully and divinely envisioned.

Notes

WRITE YOUR OWN PERSONAL STATEMENT,
(see the back of the book for note paper)

_____
_____
_____
_____
_____
_____
_____
_____
_____

Craft Your Sacred Self-Love Contract

Create a personal self-love contract that serves as a daily reminder of your commitment to cherishing and honoring yourself as the divine being you are.

1. Set the Space:
   - Find a quiet, comfortable place where you can reflect without distractions. You may want to light a candle, play calming music, or meditate for a few minutes to center yourself.
   - Have your journal, a piece of paper, or a decorative card ready, along with your favorite pen or markers.
2. Reflection:
   - Close your eyes and take a few deep breaths. Reflect on what it means for you to love, honor, and cherish yourself. Think about the qualities that make you feel most aligned with your inner goddess.
   - Consider the ways you currently show love to yourself and areas where you want to deepen your self-care practice.
3. Write Your Contract:
   - Begin by addressing yourself in a loving and affirming way. You can use phrases such as "I, [Your Name], honor the goddess within me..." or "As a divine being, I vow to..."
   - Write down the promises you are making to yourself. These might include some of the ritual from this book or affirmative statements like:
     - "I promise to take care of my body through rest, nourishment, and movement."
     - "I commit to nurturing my emotions with kindness and allowing myself to feel fully."
     - "I will speak to myself with love, recognizing that I am worthy of respect, love, and joy."
     - "I vow to honor my boundaries and protect my energy by saying no when necessary."
     - "I will seek growth, wisdom, and healing, honoring my journey without judgment."
4. Seal Your Commitment:
   - Sign your contract with your name and the date. If it feels right, add a personal mantra, affirmation, or a symbol that represents your divine nature.
5. Display Your Sacred Contract:
   - Place your contract somewhere you will see it daily. It could be on your mirror, by your bed, or in your sacred space. The goal is for it to be a divine reminder of your commitment to yourself each day.
   - Whenever you see it, take a moment to read it or repeat your mantra, reconnecting with your intention to love and honor yourself.
6. Bonus: Creative Embellishments
   - Add decorations to your contract. You can draw symbols, flowers, or patterns that feel sacred to you. Use colors that resonate with your spirit or incorporate glitter, stickers, or meaningful quotes that inspire you.

Reflection Questions:
- How does writing this contract make you feel about your relationship with yourself?
- What promises are you most excited to uphold?
- How will you check in with yourself to ensure you are honoring this commitment?

Self-love Mantra

I am the embodiment of divine love and grace. I honor my unique essence and celebrate my inner goddess. My spirit radiates beauty, strength, and wisdom. I cherish and nurture my sacred self, knowing I am worthy of infinite love and boundless joy.

Defining RADICAL SELF-LOVE

Embracing Radical Self-Love is an empowering journey of cultivating an unyielding devotion to self-care and inner harmony, transcending external circumstances. It encompasses a life philosophy that lays the groundwork for our aspirations and the connections to the collective strength inherent in all beings.

At its core, Radical Self-Love is about taking full responsibility for our emotional and physical well-being, nurturing ourselves with kindness, and initiating positive transformations. It calls us to consciously prioritize activities that uplift our spirits, bring fulfillment, and align with our purpose. Moreover, it beckons us to embrace our vulnerabilities, imperfections, and past mistakes with self-acceptance and grace.

Central to Radical Self-Love is the cultivation of authentic connections—with others and ourselves—rooted in the unwavering belief that we are deserving of love unconditionally. This transformative journey also involves forging a profound bond with nature, as spending time outdoors offers healing balm for our physical and emotional wounds, reducing stress, and granting us clarity and perspective.

In essence, Radical Self-Love is a sacred practice of nurturing our souls through life's ebb and flow, fostering resilience amid challenges and celebrating joyous moments. As we fortify this inner sanctuary, we unlock the immense power of our true essence, paving the way for profound self-understanding and boundless love, both for ourselves and others.

My List of GODDESS AFFIRMATION

Beloved Goddess, endeavor to weave each of these powerful words into a tapestry of self-love and positivity. Use them in your affirmations, journal prompts, or simply note them down in a beautifully descriptive sentence. Let each word illuminate your divine essence and elevate your spirit. Embrace your radiant self with these sacred expressions of positivity.

AWESOME	Beautiful	EXQUISITE	Capable
Great	DESIRABLE	Irreplaceable	GORGEOUS
BLESSED	Kind	HOPEFUL	Loved
Needed	INSPIRING	Magical	FANTASTIC
JOYFUL	Outstanding	Evolving	Healthy
Strong	TALENTED	Unstoppable	Witty
Grateful	OPTIMISTIC	Bright	Brave
Brilliant	Happy	CHARMING	KISSABLE
THRIVING	ADORED	CLEVER	Wise
Miracle	WONDERFUL	Independent	RESILIENT
DESERVING	Cherish	ZESTFUL	Admire
Knowledgeable	LUCKY	Dynamic	EXCELLENT
FAITH	Growth	VALUABLE	Worthy
Courageous	FABULOUS	Fearless	SMART
Opportunity	POWERFUL	EMPOWERED	Easy
LIKABLE	Motivated	INTERESTING	SWEET

Live, Laugh and Love

things I love ABOUT ME

Step 1: Honor Your Divine Beauty Write down the highest, most radiant opinion you hold about yourself. Be as specific and detailed as possible. For instance: "I possess enchanting eyes. They shimmer and change color with my moods, framed by long, fluttering eyelashes."

Step 2: Speak Your Sacred Truth Read aloud what you have written. Release any feelings of awkwardness or self-consciousness. This is your sacred moment of self-recognition.

Step 3: Envision Your Radiance Close your eyes and repeat your affirmations. As you do, visualize each cherished attribute as if you are gazing into a mirror, seeing your divine reflection.

Step 4: Transform Negativity with Light Should a shadow of doubt or negativity arise, acknowledge it with grace, then gently transform it with a positive, affirming thought. Let your inner light guide you back to self-love.

Step 5: Manifest Adoration from Others In your mind's eye, envision others recognizing and admiring your positive attributes. See them offering genuine compliments or expressing admiration in conversation, basking in the glory of your chosen qualities.

My Highest Opinion About Myself

1:

2:

3:

Mental Health Break:

Reflection:

You have reached the end of this journey, goddess!

How do you feel? What shifts have you noticed within your mind, body, and soul? Acknowledge any reflections or emotions that surface as you continue your journey of radical self-love.

How do you want to continue?

Grab a cup of tea and let your mind be free!

Prayer Affirmations

A reimagined version of Psalm 19:14

"May the words I speak and the meditations of my heart rise as sacred offerings, aligned with the divine light within me, resonating with the eternal harmony of the Universe."

SUPPORT AND PROTECTION

A reimagined version of Psalm 20:5

"May you dance with joy in the triumph of your heart's desires and may your spirit soar in the radiance of your victories. Together, we will lift our voices in celebration, calling upon the divine with the strength of our purpose fulfilled."

FOR THE COLLECTIVE

A reimagined version of Psalm 27:1-3

"The Divine Light of the Goddess shines within me; whom shall, I fear? Her strength is my foundation; of what shall I be afraid? When shadows of doubt and darkness rise against me, they shall falter before the radiant power of my sacred essence. Even if the world surrounds me in turmoil, my heart remains fearless, for I stand firm in the embrace of the Goddess, who guides my every step."

CONFIDENCE IN CONSCIOUSNESS

A reimagined version of Psalm 1

"Blessed is she who walks in harmony with divine wisdom, who does not tread the path of shadows, nor lingers in the company of those who forsake their inner light.

She finds her delight in the sacred teachings of the Goddess, and upon this wisdom, she meditates day and night.

She is like a tree, firmly rooted by streams of life-giving waters, flourishing in her season, her leaves never withering, for all she touches prospers under the watchful gaze of the Divine Mother.

But those who forsake their inner goddess are like chaff blown away by the winds of chaos, lacking the groundedness that true wisdom provides.

They shall not stand in the presence of the enlightened, nor find refuge in the circle of the divine, for their path is one of disconnection and loss.

The Goddess watches over the path of the righteous, guiding them toward their true purpose, but the way of the disconnected shall fade into obscurity."

PROTECTION

Reflection NOTES

Reflection NOTES

Reflection NOTES

Reflection NOTES

Reflection NOTES

Reflection NOTES

Self Love

DAILY TASK

DATE :

PERSONAL REMINDER

TOP PRIORITIES

INSPIRING QUOTE

AFFIRMATIONS

PERSONAL NOTES

Self Love

DAILY TASK

DATE :

PERSONAL REMINDER

TOP PRIORITIES

INSPIRING QUOTE

AFFIRMATIONS

PERSONAL NOTES

Self Love

DATE :

DAILY TASK

PERSONAL REMINDER

TOP PRIORITIES

INSPIRING QUOTE

AFFIRMATIONS

PERSONAL NOTES

Self Love

DATE :

DAILY TASK

PERSONAL REMINDER

TOP PRIORITIES

INSPIRING QUOTE

AFFIRMATIONS

PERSONAL NOTES

Self Love

DATE :

DAILY TASK

PERSONAL REMINDER

TOP PRIORITIES

INSPIRING QUOTE

AFFIRMATIONS

PERSONAL NOTES

Self Love

DAILY TASK

DATE :

PERSONAL REMINDER

TOP PRIORITIES

INSPIRING QUOTE

AFFIRMATIONS

PERSONAL NOTES

SMART GOALS

Instructions: For each goal, fill in the details according to the SMART criteria. This will help ensure that your goals are clear, focused, and actionable.

S	SPECIFIC	A. What is the divine vision you seek to manifest? B. Who are the sacred souls that will join or support you on this journey? C. Where will this sacred unfolding take place? D. Why does this intention hold profound importance in your sacred path?
M	MEASURABLE	A. How will you weave the tapestry of your progress, ensuring each thread reflects your journey? B. What sacred signs or divine markers will reveal your alignment with the path? C. How will you recognize the moment when your intention has fully blossomed?
A	ACHIEVABLE	A. Are your ambitions aligned with the divine resources at your disposal, and the sacred limitations of your current path? B. What divine actions or sacred rituals will you perform to manifest your goal? C. Do you possess the essential skills and the support of your divine circle to achieve this goal?
R	RELEVANT	A. Does this goal harmonize with the divine vision of your business and its sacred objectives? B. Will this pursuit nurture your long-term growth and the flourishing of your spiritual and material success? C. Is this the opportune moment in your sacred journey to embark on this goal?
T	TIME-BOUND	A. When will you begin to weave the threads of this sacred goal into your journey? B. What is the divine moment you envision for its completion? C. Are there, sacred milestones or checkpoints along this path to guide and illuminate your progress?

DATE: _____

SMART GOALS

GOAL: _____

S	
M	
A	
R	
T	

DATE: _____

SMART GOALS

GOAL: _____

- **S**
- **M**
- **A**
- **R**
- **T**

DATE: _____

SMART GOALS

GOAL: _____

- **S**
- **M**
- **A**
- **R**
- **T**

DATE: _____

SMART GOALS

GOAL: _____

S	
M	
A	
R	
T	

SWOT ANAYLSIS
EXAMPLE

STRENGTH

What are your strengths?

Resilience
Divine Intuition
Goal Oriented

WEAKNESS

What are your weaknesses?

Overextension
Perfectionism

SWOT

OPPORTUNITIES

What opportunities are available to you?

THREATS

What trends or conditions may negatively impact you?

SWOT ANAYLSIS

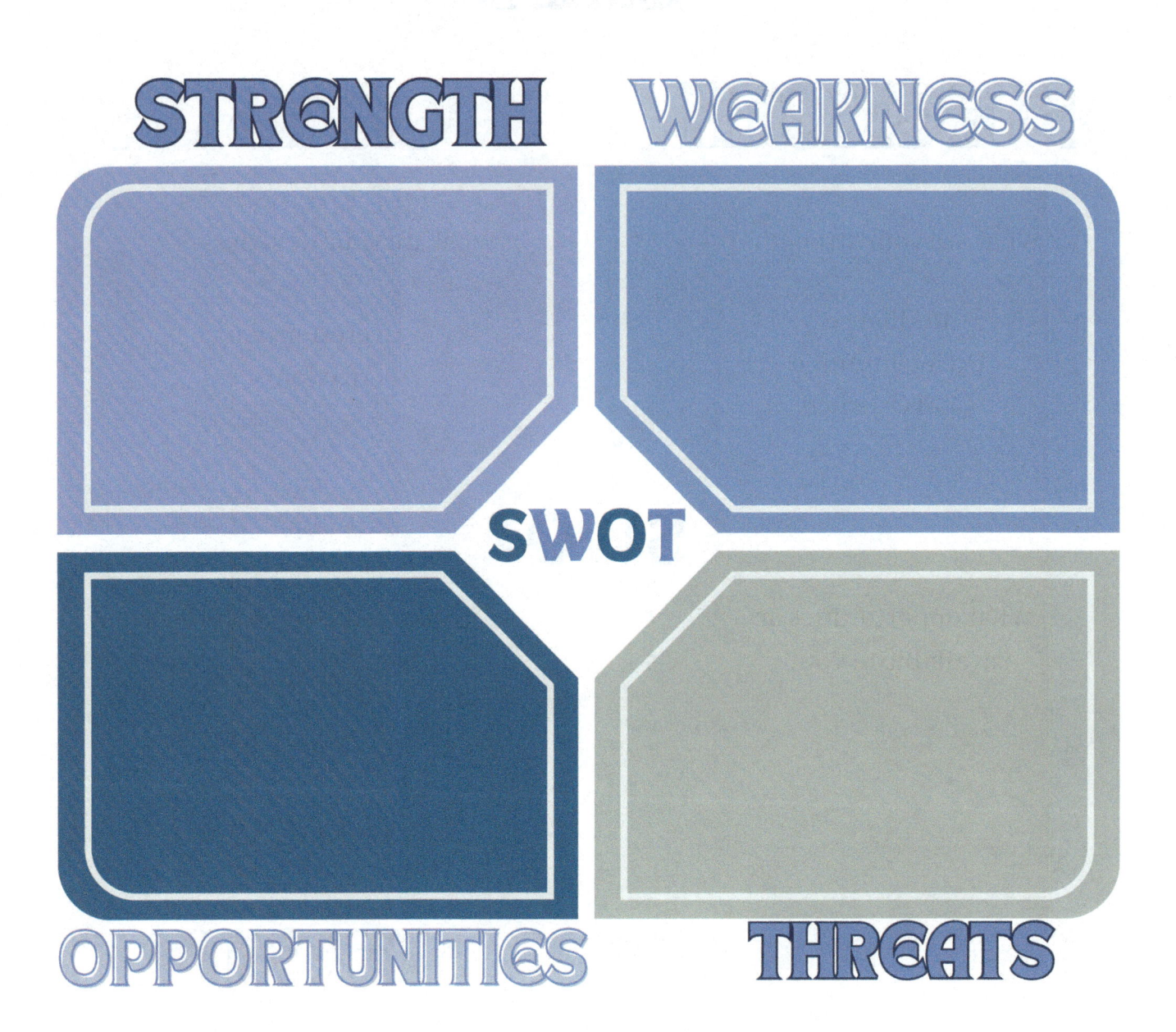

STRENGTH

WEAKNESS

SWOT

OPPORTUNITIES

THREATS

top 5 New Habits

Jan	Feb	Mar	Apr
May	Jun	Jul	Aug
Sep	Oct	Nov	Dec

HABIT TRACKER

top 5 New Habits

Jan	Feb	Mar	Apr
May	Jun	Jul	Aug
Sep	Oct	Nov	Dec

HABIT TRACKER

top 5 New Habits

Jan	Feb	Mar	Apr
May	Jun	Jul	Aug
Sep	Oct	Nov	Dec

HABIT TRACKER

top 5 New Habits

Jan	Feb	Mar	Apr
May	Jun	Jul	Aug
Sep	Oct	Nov	Dec

HABIT TRACKER

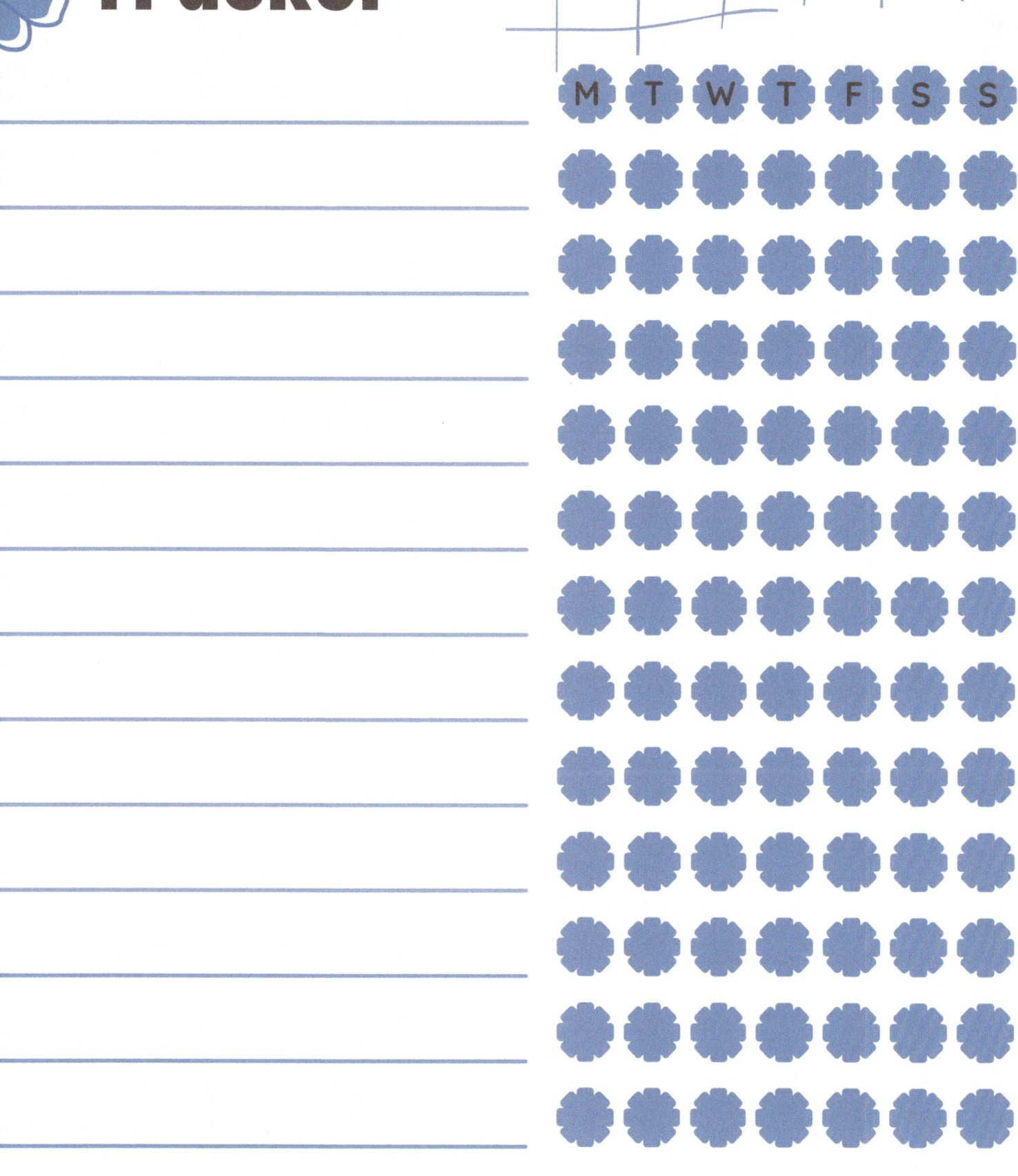

Habit Tracker

Date :

M T W T F S S

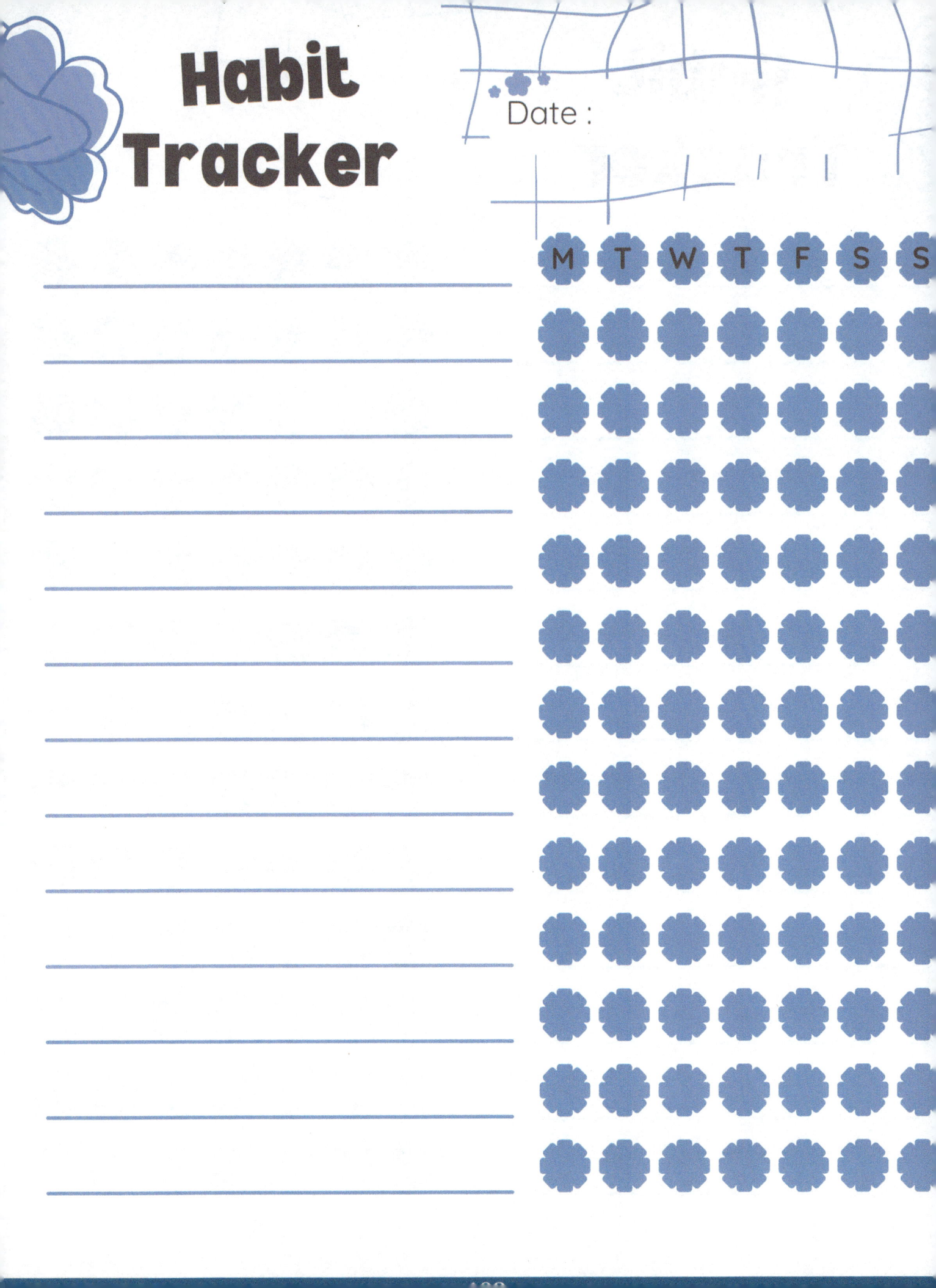

Habit Tracker

Date :

M T W T F S S

Habit Tracker

Date:

M	T	W	T	F	S	S

Habit Tracker

Date :

M	T	W	T	F	S	S

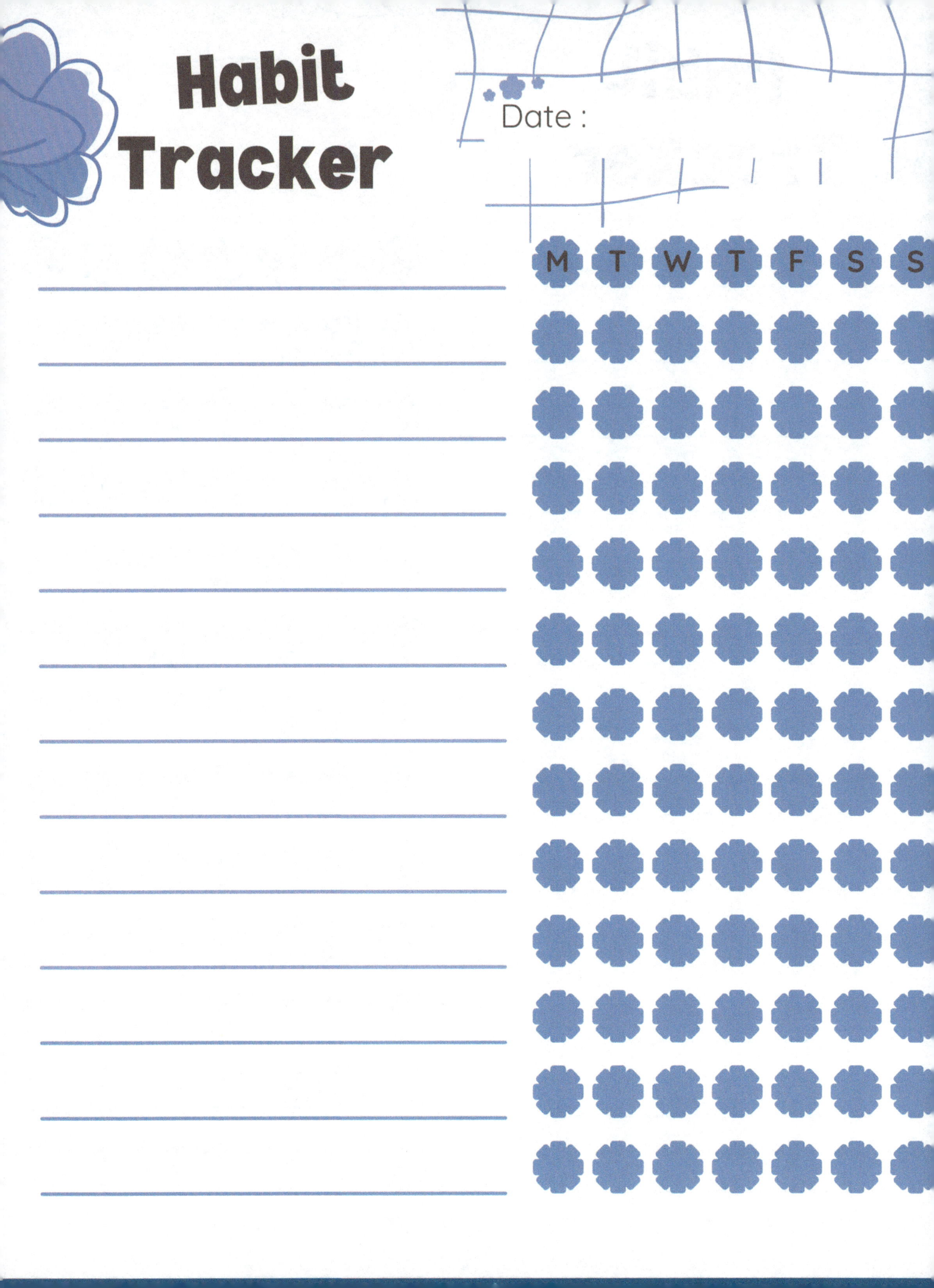

Affirmations

Here are 50 Radical Self-Love Affirmations infused with divine energy and a tone that reflects the wisdom and empowerment of a goddess:

- With each step, I move closer to my truth. With each breath, I rise.
- I am a radiant being of divine love.
- My self-love is my greatest power.
- I honor my light and my darkness.
- I am worthy of love, exactly as I am.
- I embrace my imperfections with grace.
- My soul is full of limitless possibilities.
- I am the embodiment of divine beauty.
- My worth is inherent, eternal, and unshakable.
- I honor my body as the sacred temple it is.
- I release all doubts and insecurities about my divine essence.
- My love for myself heals and transforms me.
- I trust my intuition and inner wisdom.
- I am deserving of all the abundance and joy the universe has to offer.
- My life is a reflection of my deep self-respect.
- I love and accept every part of myself.
- I am powerful beyond measure.
- My heart is open, and I receive love in all its forms.
- I embrace my past, for it shaped the goddess I am today.
- My inner peace is sacred and unshakable.
- I am a magnet for love, abundance, and divine opportunities.
- I honor the sacredness of my emotions.
- I am aligned with the highest version of myself.
- I give myself permission to rest and recharge.
- I am a masterpiece, a work of divine creation.
- My boundaries are an expression of my self-love.
- I deserve unconditional love, and I give it to myself freely.
- I trust in the divine timing of my life.
- I let go of anything that no longer aligns with my highest good.
- I celebrate my unique beauty and power.

Affirmations Cont.

- I am a vessel of love, wisdom, and divine light.
- I am at peace with myself, and my life reflects that peace.
- I choose to see myself through the eyes of love.
- I am in control of my happiness and fulfillment.
- My love for myself radiates into everything I do.
- I release all fear and step into my full power.
- I embrace change as a natural part of my growth.
- I am connected to the divine wisdom of the universe.
- I am love, I am light, I am infinite potential.
- I honor my body, mind, and spirit with tender care.
- I am my own greatest source of love, peace, and strength.
- I forgive myself for any perceived mistakes.
- I honor my journey and the lessons it has brought me.
- I am in complete harmony with my soul's purpose.
- My self-worth is not tied to external validation.
- I am a goddess, strong, wise, and full of grace.
- I allow love to flow freely to and from me.
- My voice is powerful, and I speak my truth with clarity.
- I release any guilt or shame that no longer serves me.
- I choose joy, peace, and freedom every day.
- My heart overflows with gratitude for who I am.

ABOUT *tanisha*

Greetings, Divine Beings,

I am Tanisha Scorza, the visionary soul behind Tender Love Support, LLC—a sacred sanctuary devoted to the divine alchemy of healing trauma and nurturing the essence of self-love. My being is steeped in the sacred art of catalyzing profound transformations in consciousness, all while radiating empathy and boundless compassion.

As an empath, spiritual guide, nurturer, and now an author, my life's journey has been adorned with the radiant jewels of lived experience. I cherished a sacred 23-year union, brought forth three children, and gracefully delivered two surrogate daughters, embodying the divine essence of creation and nurturing those flows through the goddess within me.

My evolutionary journey has many paths, but in this lifetime, I have chosen to walk the road less traveled. As a first-generation non-traditional college graduate, my journey toward uncovering and healing toxic patterns truly began during my time at San Diego State University, where I majored in Women's Studies and minored in Counseling as Social Change. This sacred education illuminated my path, allowing me to traverse realms and forge connections with countless souls, each encounter guiding me closer to the divine truth of Radical Self-Love.

Through my own metamorphosis, emerging from the cocoon of toxic thoughts, beliefs and behaviors, I have gathered the wisdom and strength to guide you on your sacred voyage toward healing. My existence is an ode to the transformative power of self-love.

With great delight, I unveil this workbook—a creation birthed from the depths of my soul's yearning to embody and share the teachings that have shaped my journey. Welcome to a path of profound healing and self-discovery.

Tender Love Support, always,
Tanisha Duke-Scorza

Website: www.tenderlovesupport.com

Speak your truth, and let your divine light shine.

Continue your Journey

Contact Us at

www.tenderlovesupport.com

We offer additional support:

Step into Your Divine Power

Connect with me through our Quick Conversation. These sessions offer a fast and effective way for individuals to address immediate concerns or discover deeper emotional needs. These brief yet powerful discussions provide clarity and guidance, helping you resolve pressing issues or understand what areas of your life may benefit from ongoing therapeutic support.

Embrace Your Divine Guidance

We recognize the emotional demands placed on professionals in the mental health and social service fields. Our Healing Circles are designed to offer a safe and rejuvenating space for therapists, case managers, and other client-centered professionals. These circles foster community, encourage self-care, and provide a restorative environment to help you continue the important work you do.

Discover More on Our Website

In addition to our Quick Conversation sessions, we invite you to explore the inspirational blogs and carefully curated merchandise available on our site. Our blogs are designed to uplift, motivate, and support you on your journey toward healing and self-discovery. Meanwhile, our merchandise serves as a reminder of your personal growth and divine power, offering tools and products that align with your path toward emotional well-being and empowerment.

Made in the USA
Monee, IL
29 May 2025